9/11

THE BIG LIE

Thierry Meyssan

Title page photograph : SIPA - Associated Press
Photograph Tom Horan

Library of Congress Cataloging-in-Publication Data:
Meyssan, Thierry.
[Effroyable imposture. English]
The big lie : the Pentagon plane crash that never happened /
Thierry Meyssan.
p.cm.
Translation of: L'Effroyable imposture.
Includes bibliographical references.
ISBN 1-59209-026-5
1. American Airlines Flight 77 Hijacking Incident, 2001. 2. Terrorism — Government policy—United States
I. Title
HV6432.7.M4913 2002
975.5'295044—dc21
2002010998

Carnot Publishing Ltd
20/22 Bedford Row
London WC 1R 4JS
United Kingdom

DISCLAIMER

This publication contains the opinions and ideas of its authors.

It is intended to provide helpful and informative material on the subject matter covered. It is sold with the understanding that the author and publisher are not engaged in rendering professional services in the book. If the reader requires personal assistance or advice, a competent professional should be consulted.

The author and publisher specifically disclaim any responsibility for any liability, loss, or risk, personal or otherwise, which is incurred as a consequence, directly or indirectly, of the use and application of any of the contents of this book.

NOTICE

The official documents quoted are available at the Internet addresses indicated in the footnotes.

In the event that they are removed from US-based sites, they have also been regrouped and archived at http://www.effroyable-imposture.net, where readers may readily consult them.

INTRODUCTION

The events of 11 September 2001 were followed live by hundreds of millions of people riveted to their television screens that day. All of those watching, including television commentators, were badly shaken, stunned by the scale of the attack and shocked by its gratuitous violence. The initial lack of information as to the response of the American authorities as well as the spectacular violence of the images led the TV networks to broadcast over and over again shots of the suicide planes colliding into the Twin Towers of the World Trade Center and the subsequent building collapses. The constraints of live broadcasting combined with the element of surprise limited reporting to the description of the bare facts as they became known and did not allow any general understanding of the situation.

During the three days which followed the attacks, a considerable amount of supplementary information as to some of the more obscure aspects of these events was released to the press by government officials. But it tended to be drowned out in the uninterrupted flood of news concerning the victims and rescue operations. Other items appeared sporadically in the course of later months, in an anecdotal fashion without any attempt to place them within a general context.

Several thousand people lost their lives on September 11 and a war was waged in Afghanistan to avenge them. Yet the events themselves remain mysterious. The accounts available are filled with oddities, uncertainties and contradictions. Despite the unease these anomalies provoke, public opinion has contented itself with the official version, accepting that national security imperatives prevent United States authorities from revealing the full story.

But this official version does not stand up to critical analysis. We will demonstrate that it is nothing more than a cover-up. In some instances, the elements that we have gathered allow the truth to be restored. In others, our questions remain for the moment unanswered, but this is no reason to go on believing the lies put forward by officials. In any case, the investigation that we have carried out is already sufficient to undermine the legitimacy of America's riposte in Afghanistan and its *"war on the Evil Axis"*.

We are not asking you to consider our work as the definitive truth. On the contrary, we welcome your skepticism. Don't trust anything except your own critical mind. In order to let you verify our imputations and then make up your own minds, we have enriched the text with numerous footnotes indicating our principal sources.

In this period when the United States is busy sorting out Good from Evil, we strive to remind people that freedom is not belief in a simplistic vision of the world, but entails understanding, attempting to widen the options available and distinguishing multiple nuances.

PART I

A BLOODY STAGE IS SET

Chapter 1

THE PENTAGON'S PHANTOM PLANE

Remember the attack on the Pentagon? Events that day were so momentous and so sudden that it was impossible at the time to take notice of the contradictions in the official version of what happened.

On September 11, 2001, shortly before 10 am Washington time, the Department of Defense issued a brief announcement: *"The Department of Defense is continuing to respond to the attack that occurred this morning at 9:38 am EDT. There are no casualty figures currently available. Injured personnel were taken to several area hospitals. Secretary of Defense Donald H. Rumsfeld has expressed his concern for the families of those killed and injured during this shameless attack and is directing operations from his command center in the Pentagon. All personnel were evacuated from the building as emergency response personnel from the Department of Defense and surrounding communities responded to fire and medical emergencies. Initial estimates of the damage are significant; however, the Pentagon is expected to be reopened tomorrow morning. Alternate worksites for those affected parts of the building are currently being identified."*[1]

First on the scene, Reuters news agency announced that the Pentagon had suffered damage from a helicopter explosion. This news was confirmed by a telephone call to Associated Press[2] from a Democratic Party consultant, Paul Begala. A few minutes later, the Department of Defense corrected its information, saying that a plane was involved. New eyewitness accounts emerged contradicting the first ones and supporting the official version: Fred Hay[3], an assistant to Senator Bob Ney, saw a Boeing aircraft fall as he was driving along the highway adjacent to the Pentagon. Senator Mark Kirk[4] was leaving the Pentagon's parking lot, after a breakfast with the Defense Secretary, when a large plane crashed. The Secretary himself, Donald Rumsfeld, left his office and hurried over to the crash site to help with rescue efforts.

The Arlington County firemen intervened, and were joined by four teams from the Federal Emergency Management Agency (FEMA) as well as specialist firefighters from Reagan airport. At about 10:10 am, the wing of the Pentagon that had been hit collapsed.

Members of the press was kept away from the scene in order not to hinder rescue operations and had to content themselves with filming the first body bags that were aligned in silence at a improvised field hospital. But the Associated Press managed to obtain photos of the firefighters' arrival, taken by a private individual from a nearby building.

In the confusion, it would be several hours before the newly designated Chairman of the Joint Chiefs of Staff, General Richard Myers, indicated that the *"suicide plane"* was the Boeing 757-200 from American Airlines Flight 77, which had departed Dulles airport in Washington D.C. bound for Los Angeles, before air traffic controllers lost its trace at 8:55 am. The press agencies, still scrambling to cover the story, heightened tension by reporting nearly eight hundred dead. This figure turned out to be wildly inaccurate, although Defense Secretary Donald Rumsfeld refrained from correcting it at his press conference the following day, when a more precise death toll, fortunately only a quarter of the initial press estimates, was already known.[5]

To the entire world, following on the attacks on the World Trade Center, it was an additional shock: the most powerful army in the world had been unable to protect its own headquarters and had suffered heavy losses. The United States, which had hitherto seemed invincible, were vulnerable even on their own soil.

* * *

At first sight, the facts are indisputable. And yet, once one goes into the details, the official explanations become embarrassingly contradictory.

The air traffic controllers working for the Federal Aviation Administration (FAA) told reporters from the *Christian Science Monitor*[6] that, at around 8:55 am, the Boeing descended to 29,000 feet and had not responded to their instructions. Its transponder then went silent, leading the controllers to assume at first that an electrical failure had affected the plane's flight systems. But the pilot, who had still not responded to their calls, intermittently turned on his radio, allowing them to hear a voice with a strong Arab accent who was threatening him. The plane at that point turned back towards Washington, after which they lost its trace.

In accordance with pre-established procedures, the local air traffic controllers notified the hijacking to FAA headquarters. Most of the agency's chiefs were absent, away in Canada attending a professional conference. In the midst of the panic that day, the staff on duty at FAA headquarters believed that this message was yet another notification concerning the second plane which had been diverted to New York City. It was not before another half-hour had passed that they finally realized that a third hijacking had taken place and informed the military authorities. This misunderstanding wasted twenty-nine precious minutes.

Questioned on 13 September by the Senate Armed Services Committee, the Chairman of the Joint Chiefs of Staff, General Richard Myers[7], was unable to report on the measures taken to intercept the Boeing. From this animated exchange with America's top-ranking military officer, the senators concluded that no attempt at interception had been initiated (see the excerpt from the hearing included in the Documents & Appendices section at the end of this book). But are we really to believe that the armed forces of the United States remained passive during the attacks?

To counter the disastrous effect of this hearing, the North American Aerospace Defense Command (NORAD) issued a press release[8] on September 14. Filling in the gaps of General Myers's memory, NORAD claimed it only received warning of the hijacking at 9:24 am, and assured that it had immediately ordered two F-16 fighters from the Langley Air Force base in Virginia to intercept the Boeing. But the Air Force, not knowing its exact location, believed the plane was on its way to commit a third strike against New York and sent its fighters northwards. A military transport plane, taking off from the Presidential base at Saint Andrews, spotted the Boeing by pure chance and identified it. But it was too late.

It's not clear that NORAD's version of events is any more creditable that that of the Chairman of the Joint Chiefs of Staff. How can we believe that the U.S. military's radar system was incapable of locating a Boeing within a zone of only a few dozen miles in radius? Or that a big jetliner could elude two fighters launched in its pursuit?

Even supposing that the Boeing managed to overcome this first obstacle, it should have been shot down while approaching the Pentagon. The security arrangements protecting the Department of Defense are of course a military secret, as are those concerning the White House nearby. It is known that the systems were revised[9] after a series of incidents that occurred in 1994, notably the landing of a small airplane, a Cessna 150L, on the White House lawn. We also know that these anti-aircraft defenses include five batteries of missiles installed on top of the Pentagon and fighters stationed at the Presidential airbase of Saint Andrews.[10] Two fighter squadrons are permanently based there: the Air Force's 113th Fighter Wing and the Navy's 321st Fighter Attack Wing. Equipped respectively with F-16's and F/A-18's, they should never have let the Boeing approach the Pentagon.

But as the Pentagon spokesman, Lieutenant-Colonel Vic Warzinski, put it, *"The Pentagon was simply not aware that this aircraft was coming our way, and I doubt prior to Tuesday's events, anyone would have expected anything like that here."*[11]

Having thus managed to throw its pursuers off track and penetrate the most sophisticated anti-aircraft system in the world without a scratch, the Boeing finished its flight at the Pentagon.

A Boeing 757-200[12] is a carrier capable of transporting 239 passengers. It measures 155 feet long, with a wingspan of 125 feet. When completely full, this monster weighs 115 tons, yet is capable of maintaining a cruising speed of 560 miles per hour.

As for the Pentagon[13], it is the world's largest administrative building. Its name stems from its original structure, composed of five concentric rings, each with five sides. It was built not very far away from the White House, but on the opposite bank of the Potomac river. It is thus not located in Washington D.C. proper, but in Arlington, Virginia.

In order to cause the greatest amount of damage, the Boeing should have dived into the Pentagon's roof. This would in fact have been the simplest course, as the building covers a surface of 29 acres. Instead, the terrorists chose to strike one of the façades, although its height was only 80 feet.

The plane suddenly approached the ground, as if to land. While remaining horizontal, it came down almost vertically, without damaging the lights along the highway that runs by the Pentagon parking lot, either through direct impact or the backwash of its passage. Only one lamppost in the parking lot itself was cut down.

The Boeing struck the building's façade at the height of the ground and first floors. It managed to do all this, as one can see in the photo on the front cover of this book, without damaging the magnificent lawn in the foreground, or the wall, or the parking lot, or the heliport (there is a landing pad for small copters close to the point of impact).

Despite its weight (a hundred tons) and its speed (between 250 and 440 mph), the plane only destroyed the first ring of the building. This can be seen quite distinctly in the photo below.

Photo credit: DoD, Tech. Sgt. Cedric H. Rudisill:

The shock was felt throughout the entire Pentagon. The plane's fuel, stored in the aircraft's wings, was set ablaze and the fire spread to the building. 125 people lost their lives, to which should be added the 64 people aboard the Boeing.

Luckily (if that can be said at all), the plane hit a section of the Pentagon that was undergoing renovation. They had just finished installing the Navy's brand new Command Center.[14] Many offices were still unoccupied and others were being used by the civilian personnel in charge of the renovation. That explains why most of the casualties were civilians, and why only one general was to be found among the military victims.

A half-hour later, the upper floors collapsed.

Photo credit: US Marine Corps, Cpl. Jason Ingersoll:
jccc.afis.osd.mil/images/sres.pl?Lbox_cap=356243&dir=Photo&vn
=&ttl=010911-M-41221-021&ref=defenselink

Photo credit: Jim Garamone, American Forces Press Service
www.defenselink.mil/news/Sep2001/n09112001_200109114.html

These first elements of the official story are very unlikely, while the rest is strictly impossible.

If one superimposes the plane's outline onto the satellite photo below, it can be seen that only the nose of the Boeing entered the building. The fuselage and the wings remained outside.

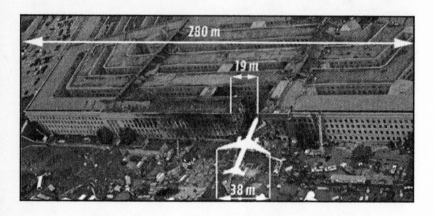

Credit: DoD, Tech. Sgt. Cedric H. Rudisill
www.defenselink.mil/photos/Sep2001/010914-F-8006R-006.html

The plane was stopped dead, without its wings having struck the façade. There is no visible trace of any impact except that from the Boeing's nose.

We should thus be able to see the wings and the fuselage outside, on the lawn in fact.

While the plane's nose is made of carbon and the wings, containing the fuel, can burn, the Boeing's fuselage is aluminum and the jet engines are built out of steel. At the end of the fire, it would necessarily have left a burnt-out wreck. If you refer to the Associated Press photo (on the front cover of this book), you will clearly observe that there is no plane. The shot was nevertheless taken in the very first minutes: the fire trucks had arrived, but the firemen had not yet deployed.

At a press conference[15] held on September 12, the Arlington County fire chief, Ed Plaugher, made it clear that his men were employed in fighting the fire's spread within the Pentagon, but had been kept away from the immediate crash site. Only the FEMA's special Urban Search and Rescue teams came into contact with the plane.

A surreal dialogue then took place during this press conference:

Reporter: *"Is there anything left of the aircraft at all?"*

Plaugher: *"First all, the question about the aircraft, there are some small pieces of aircraft visible from the interior during this fire-fighting operation I'm talking about, but not large sections. In other words, there's no fuselage sections and that sort of thing."*
[...]

Reporter: *"Chief, there are small pieces of the plane virtually all over, out over the highway, tiny pieces. Would you say the plane exploded, virtually exploded on impact due to the fuel or...?"*

Plaugher: *"You know, I'd rather not comment on that. We have a lot of eyewitnesses that can give you better information about what actually happened with the aircraft as it approached. So we don't know. I don't know."*
[...]

Reporter: *"Where is the jet fuel? Just ...?"*

Plaugher: *"We have what we believe is a puddle right there that the... what we believe is to be the nose of the aircraft"* (sic).

So, although officials, members of Congress and military personnel all claimed to have seen the aircraft fall, no one saw the smallest piece of the plane, not even from the landing gear: there were only unidentifiable metal fragments. As for the video surveillance cameras in the Pentagon parking lot, they did not see the Boeing either, at any point of time or at any angle.

To recap the official version: a hijacked Boeing eluded the F-16 fighters sent in its pursuit and foiled the anti-aircraft defense system in Washington. It landed vertically on the Pentagon parking lot while remaining in a horizontal position. It struck the façade at ground level. Its nose and fuselage are supposed to have penetrated into the building. One of its wings, perhaps both of them, burned outdoors, while the fuselage disintegrated inside. The fuel, stored in the wings, burned just long enough to start a fire in the building, and then was transformed into a puddle which moved itself to the spot where the plane's nose supposedly came to a halt.

Not withstanding the respect owed to the high rank of the "eye witnesses" – including military officers and members of Congress – it is impossible to swallow such nonsense. Far from lending credit to their depositions, their rank only underlines the importance of the means deployed by the United States army to distort the truth.

All the same, this loony tale was constructed in bits and pieces, one lie leading to another. If you refer to the Pentagon's initial press release, quoted at the beginning of this chapter, you will notice that there was no question of any Boeing. The theory of the *"kamikaze plane"* did not emerge until a half-hour later. Similarly, there was no question of any fighters trying to intercept the phantom plane at the time of the Chairman of the

Joint Chiefs of Staff's congressional hearing. It was only two days later that NORAD invented the roving F-16's.

* * *

The official version is only propaganda. But the facts remain that 125 persons died at the Pentagon and that an airplane carrying 64 passengers disappeared. What caused the explosion that damaged the Pentagon? What became of American Airlines flight 77? Are the passengers dead? If so, who killed them and why? If not, where are they? The U.S. Administration should address all these questions.

Above all, we should ask ourselves what the official version is trying to hide. Questioned by CNN the day after the attack, General Wesley Clark, former supreme commander of NATO forces during the war in Kosovo, declared, *"We have known for some time that some groups were planning* [an assault on the Pentagon], *obviously we didn't do enough* [to prepare for one]".[16] This enigmatic assertion makes no reference to a foreign aggressor, but rather to threats against the Pentagon issued by extreme right-wing militias. It allows a glimpse of the secret struggles raging with the United States' ruling class.

CNN also interviewed Hosni Mubarak on September 15.[17] At that point in time, the Egyptian president did not have the same information at his disposal that we have now. He did not know what a detailed analysis of the attack teaches us. On the other hand, he did have confidential intelligence concerning the preparations for the attack that he had transmitted several weeks earlier to the American government.

President Hosni Mubarak: "[...] *Not any intelligence in the world could have the capability in the world to say they are going to use commercial planes with passengers on board to crash the towers, to crash the Pentagon, those who did that should have flown in the area a long time, for example. The Pentagon is not very high, a pilot could come straight to the Pentagon like this to hit, he should have flown a lot in this area to know the obstacles which could meet him when he is flying very low with a big commercial plane to hit the Pentagon in a special place. Somebody has studied this very well, someone has flown in this area very much.*"

CNN: "*Are you suggesting it was an inside operation? I may ask, who do you think is behind this?*"

Mubarak: "*Frankly speaking, I don't want to jump to conclusions, you in the United States when you catch somebody, some rumors about somebody, you say* 'Oh no, it is not Egyptian, it is Saudi, it is Emirates... all this is inside any house of an Arab, the people say the Arabs are participating... you cannot foretell, it is better wait.' *You remember Oklahoma... there came rumors immediately that the Arabs did it, and it was not Arabs, who knows... let us wait and see what is the result of the investigations, because something like this done in the United States is not an easy thing for some pilots who had been training in Florida, so many pilots go and train just to fly and have a license, that means you are capable to do such terrorist action? I am speaking as a former pilot, I know that very well, I flew very heavy planes, I flew fighters, I know that very well, this is not an easy thing, so I think we should not jump to conclusions for now.*

* * *

Numerous people, who were in their cars on the highway running alongside the Pentagon, heard the sound of a plane passing overhead. This sound was shrill, like that of a fighter aircraft, not a commercial airliner. Some said they saw this aircraft. They then described it as a small plane that might have contained eight to twelve persons, not a Boeing 757.[18]

Danielle O'Brien, an air traffic controller at Dulles airport, described to ABC News the behavior of this aircraft, as seen on radar.[19] It was flying at a speed of around 500 mph and was heading at first for the protected airspace surrounding the White House and the Capitol, then veered sharply towards the Pentagon. For O'Brien and her colleagues, there was no possible doubt: given its speed and manoeuvrability, it could not be a commercial airliner, but only a military aircraft.

The aircraft penetrated the building without causing major damage to the façade. It traversed several rings of the Pentagon, opening successively wider holes in each partition as it passed. The final orifice, perfectly circular in form, measured roughly seven feet in diameter. In traversing the Pentagon's first ring, the aircraft started a fire, as gigantic as it was sudden. Immense flames issued from the building, licking at the façades. They withdrew just as quickly, leaving behind them a cloud of black soot. The fire spread within a section of the first ring and in two perpendicular corridors. It was so sudden that the building's fire protection devices were ineffective.

All of this testimony and these observations could correspond with the firing of one of the latest generation of AGM-type missiles, armed with a hollow charge and a depleted uranium BLU tip, and guided by GPS. This kind of weapon does look like a small civilian airplane, but it's not a plane at all. It produces a whistling noise similar to that of a fighter aircraft, can be guided precisely enough to enter a building by a window, can pierce the toughest armor, and can cause – independently of its armor-piercing effect – an instantaneous fire giving off heat in excess of 3,600° Fahrenheit.

That being said, only a missile of the United States armed forces transmitting a friendly code could enter the Pentagon's airspace without provoking a counter-missile barrage. This attack could only be committed by United States military personnel against other U.S. military personnel.

* * *

If the Bush Administration faked the attack on the Pentagon to cover up certain internal problems, did it also dissemble concerning some elements of the attacks that occurred at the World Trade Center?

Chapter 2

ACCOMPLICES ON THE GROUND

Let's remember how the attacks in New York were originally presented. On Tuesday, September 11, 2001, at 8:50 am, the 24-hour television news network, CNN, interrupted its programs to announce that an airliner has hit the north tower of the World Trade Center. As it did not have pictures of the catastrophe, it broadcast a fixed shot of the Manhattan skyline that allowed viewers to see the smoke billowing from the tower.

At first, it was thought to be a spectacular accident. The American air transport companies, on the verge of bankruptcy, maintain their fleets ever more poorly. Air traffic controllers provide an unreliable service. Spreading deregulation has allowed anarchic over-flights of urban areas. So what was bound to occur finally happened.

Nevertheless, the possibility that it wasn't an accident could not be ruled out, as CNN wasted no time in pointing out. It would then be the result of terrorist action. There was the precedent of February 26, 1993, when a van with explosives detonated in the sub-basement level of the World Trade Center's parking lot, killing six people and injuring a thousand others. The attack was attributed to a militant Islamic organization led, from New York itself, by Sheikh Omar Abdul Rahman. According to CNN's commentators, if the crash was an attack, it was probably the work of another Islamic fundamentalist, the former Saudi millionaire, Osama bin Laden. In a *fatwah* dated 23 August 1996, this financier, who had taken refuge in Afghanistan, called for a holy war against the United States and Israel. The attacks perpetrated on August 7, 1998 against the American embassies in Nairobi (Kenya) and Dar-es-Salaam (Tanzania) were attributed to him. In the space of a few years he had become *"Public Enemy N° 1 of the United States"* The FBI had offered a price on his head of five million dollars. The Security Council at the United Nations had demanded his extradition from the Taliban government. Since February 5, 2001, the United States had in fact been pursuing his trial *in absentia*, in a New York court.

One after another, the American television networks set up live coverage from New York City. At 9:03 am, a second airliner hit the south tower of the World Trade Center. The crash happened as numerous networks were broadcasting pictures of the north tower in flames. It was thus filmed from several angles and seen live by millions of television viewers. It became obvious that the United States was faced with terrorist actions on their own soil. Fearing car bomb attacks, the New York Port Authority closed traffic on all of the bridges and tunnels in Manhattan (and there were even those scared of ground commandos!). At 9:40 am, the New York police informed the population that more planes might strike other towers. At 10:00 am, when the attack on the Pentagon had just been announced, the south tower of the WTC collapsed live on television screens, then at 10:29

am, it was the turn of the north tower. A cloud of dust blanketed Manhattan. The possibility of a death toll totaling several tens of thousands was raised. The combustion of the airplanes had created a heat so intense that the metallic structures of the buildings had been unable to withstand it.

The Governor of New York, George Pataki, closed all State offices and called up the National Guard. *"I have friends in those towers, my thoughts are for them, and we will try to bring support to all those who are touched by this tragedy,"* he confided. At 11:02 am, the mayor of New York City, Rudolph Giuliani, speaking by telephone to New York One radio, addressed the city's population. *"To those who are not in Manhattan, stay at home or at the office. If you are in the business district, walk calmly to the north, away from the area of the attack, in order not to interfere rescue operations. We should try to save as many people as possible."* A dense crowd of several tens of thousands of people then crossed the bridges (they were already closed to automobile traffic), fleeing Manhattan.

At 5:20 pm, building 7 of the World Trade Center, which had not been hit by the planes, also collapsed, without any further casualties. The New York emergency services thought the building had been damaged by the two previous collapses. Through a sort of domino effect, other neighboring buildings were liable to fall in turn. New York's City Hall ordered thirty thousand body bags.

During the afternoon and the days that followed, the attack's scenario was reconstituted: Islamic militants belonging to bin Laden's networks, organized in teams of five and armed with cutters had taken control of the airliners. Fanatics, they sacrificed themselves by flying their kamikaze planes into the buildings.

* * *

At first sight, the facts are unassailable. But yet again, the more one delves into the details, the more contradictions surface.

The two planes were identified by the FBI as Boeing 767's, the first belonging to American Airlines (flight 11, Boston-Los Angeles) and the second to United Airlines (flight 175, Boston-Los Angeles). The companies have admitted losing these planes.

Thanks to passengers carrying cellular phones who called family or friends during the operation, it is known that the hijackers herded the passengers to the rear of the planes, a classic means of isolating the cockpit. Their action was facilitated by the small number of passengers: 81 on flight 11 and 56 on flight 175 for 239 seats on each plane.

According to the information provided over telephone by the passengers, the hijackers only carried sharp-edged weapons.[20] Once United States airspace was closed down, all planes in flight were told to land and were searched by the FBI. In two cases, flight 43 (Newark-Los Angeles) and flight 1729 (Newark-San Francisco) identical cutters were discovered hidden under seats. Investigators surmised that all of the hijackers used this model of cutter. Later on, the CIA discovered bags of cutters in a house where Osama bin Laden stayed in Afghanistan, attesting to the fact that Islamic militants had received training in handling them.

It is nevertheless difficult to conceive that the organizer of the attackers would have neglected to furnish his men with firearms and taken the risk of seeing his operation fail, either totally or in part. It's all the more surprising in that it's easier to pass through airport checks with adapted handguns[21] than with cutters.

Why ask such questions? In the public's collective imagination, it's a well-known fact that Arabs, and thus Islamic militants, like to slit their victim's throats. The cutters allowed people to infer that all the hijackers were Arabs, although this remains to be proven.

Before arriving in New York, the planes had to reduce their altitude considerably, so that the pilots could see the towers face-on, rather than from above. Seen from the sky, a city resembles a map and all usual visual references disappear. In order to strike the towers, the planes needed to be pre-positioned at a very low altitude.

The pilots not only had to adjust the altitude of the crashes, but also position the aircraft laterally. The width of the Twin Towers was 209 feet. The wingspan of a 767 is 156 feet. On video, one can see that the planes hit squarely in the center of their targets. A displacement of merely 183 feet would have caused the planes to miss their strike entirely. At average speed (440 mph), that distance is traveled in three-tenths of a second. Given the low maneuverability of these aircraft, that would have been a remarkable feat even for a experienced pilot, let alone trainees.

The first plane arrived perfectly face-on, with the wind behind it, which facilitated its stabilization. But the second plane was forced to execute a complex rotation maneuver, particularly difficult facing the wind. Nevertheless, it, too, struck its tower at a good height and well-centered.

The professional pilots we talked to confirmed that few amongst themselves could envisage performing such an operation and completely ruled it out in the case of amateur pilots. There is, however, one infallible method of achieving this result: the use of radio beacons. A signal, transmitted from the target, guides the plane in automatically. Now, the existence of a beacon in the World Trade Center has been attested to by radio hams who recorded its signal. It was detected because it interfered with the transmission of television antennas placed on top of the towers. It is probable that the signal was activated at the last moment so that no one could discover it and destroy it. It is possible that the hijackers used two beacons, because one alone would scarcely have done the job, despite the alignment of the two targets. In any event, they required accomplices on the ground. And if they had them, it was not necessary to have numerous hijackers on board. A small team would have sufficed to put the plane on automatic pilot. It was not necessary in fact to have any hijackers on board at all, as there was no taking of hostages: by hacking into the planes' computers before takeoff, it would have been possible to take over the aircraft in flight, thanks to the Global Hawk technology perfected by the Department of Defense.[22] The Boeing would have been under remote control, like a drone – a plane without a pilot.

After the crashes, the Twin Towers collapsed upon themselves. An investigative commission was entrusted by the Federal Emergency Management Agency (FEMA) to the American Society of Civil Engineers (ASCE). According to the preliminary report, the combustion of the planes' fuel unleashed a formidable amount of heat that weakened the central metallic structure of the two buildings.

This theory was vigorously rejected by the New York firemen's associations and the professional review, *Fire Engineering*[23], which, backed up by calculations, claimed that the structures could have resisted the fire for a long period. The firemen affirm that they heard explosions at the base of the buildings and demanded the opening of an independent investigation.[24] They wondered about substances stored in the buildings, and not finding the answer there, about criminal explosions that would implicate a ground-based team. A famous expert from the New Mexico Institute of Mining and Technology, Van Romero, claimed that the collapse could only have been causes by explosives.[25] In the face of public pressure, he later retracted.

Be that as it may, the planes' crashes do not account for the fall of a third building, tower 7. The hypothesis of a destabilization of the foundations was discarded by the American Society of Civil Engineers : tower 7 wasn't leaning over, it collapsed in upon itself. The question is no longer "was it dynamited?", but rather, "what other hypothesis can one formulate?".

A journalist's scoop that appeared in the *New York Times*[26] may shed some light here. The World Trade Center, which was believed to be a civilian target, also concealed a secret military one. Perhaps thousands of people perished because they served as its human shield. Tower 7 – but perhaps other buildings and basements as well – masked a CIA base.[27] During the 1950's it served as a base for spying on foreign delegations to the United Nations, but under Bill Clinton it had illegally extended its activities to electronic espionage of Manhattan. The principal resources of the American intelligence apparatus had been transferred from anti-Soviet espionage to economic warfare. The CIA base in New York had become the most important center of economic intelligence in the world. This reorientation of intelligence was vigorously contested by the more traditional branch of the CIA and the Joint Chiefs of Staff.

Retrospectively, one wonders whether the target of the attack on the World Center on 26 February 1993 (six dead, a thousand injured) was not in fact this secret CIA station, although it was far less developed at that point.

Knowing that at the time of the first crash, thirty to forty thousand people were usually in the Twin Towers, and that each tower had 110 stories, there were on average at least 136 persons per floor. The first Boeing struck the north tower between the 80th and 85th floors. The occupants of those floors perished immediately, either from the impact or the fire that followed. The people located in the floors above found themselves trapped, as the fire spread upwards. Some preferred to throw themselves into empty space rather than succumb to the flames. Finally, the structure collapsed. All the people in the top thirty floors were thus dead. According to our calculation of average occupancy per floor, there should have been at least 4,080 lives lost.

But according to the official total issued on 9 February 2002, the two attacks in New York resulted in 2,843 deaths (including the passengers and crew of the two Boeings, the police and firemen lost in the towers' collapses, and the buildings' users).[28] This total is far lower than the initial estimates, and suggests that, despite appearances, the attacks did not aim to produce the maximum possible deaths. On the contrary, prior intervention was required to ensure that numerous persons, at least those working on the top floors, were absent from their offices at the critical hour.

Thus, the Israeli daily, *Ha'aretz* revealed that Odigo, a leading firm in electronic communications, received anonymous messages warning of the New York attacks, two hours before they occurred. These facts were confirmed by Micha Macover, the firm's director.[29] Warnings of various types could have addressed to the occupants of north tower, even if all of them were not taken seriously in the same way.

One re-encounters here a pattern similar to that of the attack perpetrated in Oklahoma City on 19 April 1995. That day, a large portion of the civil servants working in the Alfred P. Murrah Federal Building were given a half-day off work so that the car bomb explosion only killed 168 persons. This was an attack we now know was carried out by military personnel belonging to an extreme right-wing organization which itself had been infiltrated by the FBI.[30]

In Oklahoma City, the FBI had thus let an attack go ahead about which it had been informed in advance, but had limited its scope.

Let's listen now to this strange confession from President George W. Bush, during a meeting with citizens in Orlando, Florida, on 4 December.[31]

Question: *"One thing, Mr. President, is that you have no idea how much you've done for this country. And another thing is that, how did you feel when you heard about the terrorist attack?"* (Applause.)

President George W. Bush: *"Thank you, Jordan. Well, Jordan, you're not going to believe what state I was in when I heard about the terrorist attack. I was in*

Florida. And my Chief of Staff, Andy Card — actually, I was in a classroom talking about a reading program that works. I was sitting outside the classroom waiting to go in, and I saw an airplane hit the tower — the TV was obviously on. And I used to fly, myself, and I said, well, there's one terrible pilot. I said, it must have been a horrible accident.

But I was whisked off there, I didn't have much time to think about it. And I was sitting in the classroom, and Andy Card, my Chief of Staff, who is sitting over here, walked in and said, 'A second plane has hit the tower, America is under attack.'

And, Jordan, I wasn't sure what to think at first. You know, I grew up in a period of time where the idea of America being under attack never entered my mind — just like your Daddy's and Mother's mind probably. And I started thinking hard in that very brief period of time about what it meant to be under attack. I knew that when I got all of the facts that we were under attack, there would be hell to pay for attacking America.." (Applause.)

So therefore, according to his own declaration, the President of the United States saw pictures of the first crash before the second had taken place. The pictures could not have been those accidentally filmed by French documentary-makers Jules and Gédéon Naudet. The Naudet brothers had continued filming at the World Trade Center all that day and their video was not released until thirteen hours later by Gamma agency. It must thus have been secret images transmitted to him without delay in the secure communications room that was installed in the elementary school in preparation for his visit. But if the US intelligence services could have filmed the first attack, that means they must have been informed beforehand. And in that case, why didn't they do anything to save their fellow countrymen?

To recapitulate our information: the terrorists had at their disposal logistical support teams on the ground. They activated one or two beacons, warned occupants in the towers in order to limit the human catastrophe and blew up three buildings. All of this under the eye of the intelligence services, who observed but did not intervene.

Could an operation of this nature have really been conceived and directed from a cave in Afghanistan, and then carried out by a handful of Islamic militants?

Chapter 3

MOLES IN THE WHITE HOUSE

Let's return to the official version of events on that terrible day. In response to the two attacks that occurred in New York, the FBI director, Robert Mueller III activated CONPLAN[32]: all government agencies were informed of the catastrophe and asked to place themselves at the disposal of the Strategic Information and Operations Center (SIOC) at the FBI and the Catastrophic Disaster Response Group (CDRG) at FEMA. All major public gathering sites liable to become the theater of terrorist operations were evacuated and closed.

Suddenly, at around 10 am, the Secret Service (i.e. the service protecting the highest authorities in the United States) issued a new type of alert: both the White House and Air Force One were under threat. Vice President Cheney was taken to the Presidential Emergency Operations Center (PEOC), the underground command room situated beneath the West Wing of the White House. The plan for Continuity of Government (CoG) was activated. The country's principal political leaders, members of the executive and of Congress, were transferred to safe places. Marine helicopters carried them to two gigantic nuclear bomb shelters: the High Point Special Facility (Mount Weather, Virginia) and the Alternative Joint Communication Center, also known as "Site R" (Raven Rock Mountain, near Camp David). These are veritable underground cities, vestiges of the Cold War, and were conceived to shelter thousands of people.

For his part, George W. Bush, who was en route to Washington, changed course. The Presidential plane, Air Force One, went first to the Barksdale base in Louisiana, then to Offutt Air Force Base in Nebraska. The latter is the headquarters of the US Strategic Command, i.e. the nodal point from which the nuclear deterrent force is activated. Between the two bases, the Presidential plane flew at low altitude, zigzagging, escorted by fighters. At the bases, the President crossed the landing fields in armored vehicles to avoid possible snipers.

This protective deployment around key authorities did not end until 6 pm, when George W. Bush re-boarded Air Force One to return to Washington.

Invited by Tim Russert as a guest on the NBC television program, *Meet the Press*[33], on 16 September, Vice President Dick Cheney described the alert raised by the Secret Service and the nature of the threat (see Documents & Appendices).

According to his own testimony, the Vice President was suddenly informed by his security officers that he was in danger and he was forcibly evacuated to the White House bunker. A hijacked Boeing jet, which turned out to be flight 77, was circling above Washington. Unable to find its way to the White House, it would crash into the Pentagon. While evacuating the leading figures in the government and Congress, the Secret Service was informed of another threat against Air Force One. Another hijacked plane was threatening to collide with the President's plane.

* * *

Once again, the official version fails to stand up to analysis.

The Vice President's testimony aimed at identifying the threat: suicide planes were heading towards the White House and Air Force One. He repeated the lie exposed in our first chapter: the one about flight 77 crashing into the Pentagon. He even embroidered on it by imagining the plane circling above Washington in search of a target. One struggles, however, to accept that the Secret Service, rather than activating the antiaircraft system, could only think of evacuating the Vice President to a bunker. Even more amusing, Cheney invented another plane chasing Air Force One like a horseman in a Western, seeking to collide with it in flight under the impotent eye of the U.S. Air Force.

Despite these unlikely details, this tale fails to explain the behavior at the highest levels of government. If the threat consisted of suicide planes, why protect the President from possible sniper fire, even on the landing fields of strategic military bases? How are we to believe that Islamic militants could take up positions in such well-guarded places?

Dick Cheney's testimony aimed above all to help make us forget about other statements that had been made by the White House spokesman, Ari Fleischer, and senior presidential adviser Karl Rove.[34] Their information raised questions about possible domestic leads, whereas the pro-war propaganda wants to see only foreign enemies.

The press[35] on September 12 and 13 claimed that, according to the Presidential spokesman (Ari Fleischer), the Secret Service received a message from the attackers indicating that they planned to destroy the White House and Air Force One. Even more surprisingly, according to the *New York Times*, the attackers established the credibility of their call by using the Presidential identification and transmission codes. And more astonishing still, *World Net Daily*[36], citing intelligence officers as its sources, said the attackers also had the codes of the Drug Enforcement Agency (DEA), the National Reconnaissance Office (NRO), Air Force Intelligence (AFI), Army Intelligence (AI), Naval Intelligence (NI), the Marine Corps Intelligence (MCI) and the intelligence services of the State Department and the Department of Energy. Each of these codes is known by only a very small group of officials. No one is authorized to possess several of them. Also, to accept that the attackers were in possession of them supposes either that there exists a method of cracking the codes, or that moles have infiltrated each of these intelligence bodies. Technically, it appears to be possible to reconstitute the codes of the American agencies by means of the software, Promis, that served to create them. Now, the algorithms of this software are known to have been stolen by FBI special agent Robert Hansen, who was arrested for espionage in February 2001.[37] For the former CIA director, James Woolsey, the codes were more likely to have been obtained by moles. And Woolsey, who today is a lobbyist for the opposition to Saddam Hussein, affirms that this operation was the work of the dangerous Iraqi secret services. A third hypothesis would be that the Secret Service itself was infiltrated and let itself be fooled: the attackers never had the codes, but – thanks to accomplices – they made it seem believable.

Whatever the case may be, the business of the codes reveals that there exists one or more traitors at the highest levels of the American state apparatus. It is they who might have posted snipers to shoot the President, even within the confines of the U.S. Air Force's strategic bases. And it was to protect him from their ambushes that President Bush was forced to ride in armored vehicles on the landing fields of Barksdale and Offutt.

Another aspect to consider in this affair is that it reveals the existence of parallel negotiations. If the attackers contacted the Secret Service and used secret codes to authenticate their call, it was because they had a precise objective in mind. Their message contained either a demand or an ultimatum. It stands to good reason that if one accepts that the threat had been dispelled by the end of the day, one can only conclude that President Bush negotiated with them and gave into blackmail.

With the authentication and transmission codes of the White House and Air Force One at their disposal, the attackers could usurp the authority of the President of the United States. They could give whatever orders they pleased to the armed forces, including the use of nuclear weapons. The only means allowing George W. Bush to retain control of the military was to physically hold the headquarters of the U.S. Strategic Command, at Offutt, and to personally issue orders and counter-orders from there. That's why he went there in person. His direct route proved impossible, due to lack of fuel. Air Force One, which was not designed for low altitude flight, had used up its reserves and could not be refueled in the air without exposing itself. A technical stopover was thus programmed for Barksdale, one of five backup sites for Offutt.

The matter of the codes was not the only element that disappeared from the official version. Another fact, duly noted at the time, has since been forgotten. On 11

September, at 9:42 am, ABC broadcast live images of a fire that had broken out in the White House annex, the Old Executive Building. The television network contented itself with showing a fixed shot of plumes of black smoke escaping from the building. No information has ever leaked out concerning the origin of the blaze, or its exact scale. No one has had the presumption to blame the fire on a kamikaze plane. A quarter of an hour later, the Secret Service took Dick Cheney from his office and ordered the evacuation of the White House and its annex. Sharpshooters were deployed around the Presidential residence, armed with rocket launchers and capable of repelling an assault by airborne troops. In short, they were facing a threat of a very different nature to that later described by Vice President Cheney.

Let's now reread the text of the President Bush's declaration, recorded at Barksdale and sent out in a delayed broadcast by the Pentagon at 1:04 pm:

"I want to reassure the American people that the full resources of the federal government are working to assist local authorities to save lives and to help the victims of these attacks. Make no mistake: The United States will hunt down and punish those responsible for these cowardly acts.

I've been in regular contact with the Vice President, the Secretary of Defense, the national security team and my Cabinet. We have taken all appropriate security precautions to protect the American people. Our military at home and around the world is on high alert status, and we have taken the necessary security precautions to continue the functions of your government.

We have been in touch with the leaders of

46

Congress and with world leaders to assure them that we will do whatever is necessary to protect America and Americans.

I ask the American people to join me in saying a thanks for all the folks who have been fighting hard to rescue our fellow citizens and to join me in saying a prayer for the victims and their families.

The resolve of our great nation is being tested. But make no mistake: we will show the world that we will pass this test. God bless."

What is striking in this speech is that the President carefully avoided designating attackers. He no longer used the words *"terrorism"* or *"terrorist"*. He hinted that it might be the beginning of a classic military conflict, or something else altogether. He spoke of a *"test"* that had to be passed and seemed to be announcing new catastrophes to come. Even more surprisingly, he offered no explanation for his absence from Washington, giving the impression that he had fled from a danger to which his fellow citizens remained exposed.

Ari Fleischer, the White House spokesman, gave two improvised press briefings aboard Air Force One during its long wandering. With the same meticulous care as President Bush, he, too, avoided the words *"terrorism"* and *"terrorist"*.

In such a context, one can interpret in two different ways the activation of the Continuity of Government (CoG) procedure. The simplest explanation is to consider the need to protect the President and other political leaders from the actions of traitors capable of starting a fire in the Old Executive Building and stealing the secret codes of both the Presidency and the intelligence agencies.

One might also consider whether, on the contrary, the CoG plan was put into effect not to protect political leaders from traitors, but was initiated by the traitors themselves to isolate those leaders. The account given by Vice President Dick Cheney is truly strange. He claims that men from the Secret Service seized him in his office and bundled him into the White House bunker without receiving his consent. He appeared to suggest that the same was true for the principal members of the government and of Congress. And what else is an operation where the secret services take elected officials and put them in bunkers *"for their own security"*, if not a *coup d'etat*, or at least a palace coup?

Let's summarize the elements available to us. A fire breaks out in the White House annex. Responsibility for the attacks is claimed during a phone call to the Secret Service. The attackers issue demands, or even an ultimatum, and establish their credibility by using the Presidency's own transmission and authentication codes. The Secret Service initiates the Continuity of Government procedure and puts the principal political leaders in shelters for safekeeping. President Bush negotiates during the afternoon and calm is restored by evening.

The attacks were thus not ordered by a fanatic who believed he was delivering divine punishment, but by a group present within the American state apparatus, which succeeded in dictating policy to President Bush. Rather than a *coup d'etat* aimed at overthrowing existing institutions, might it not involve instead the seizure of power by a particular group hidden within those institutions?

Chapter 4

THE FBI WRINGS ITS HANDS

With that amazing flair for organization that constitutes the hallmark of the United States, during the day of September 11 the FBI launched the biggest criminal investigation in human history: "Penttbomb" (a contraction of Pentagon-Twin Towers-Bomb). It mobilized a quarter of its personnel, seven thousand civil servants in all, including four thousand agents, for this task. To its own resources, it added those detached by other agencies within the Department of Justice: the Criminal Division, the Attorneys' Bureau, and the Immigration and Naturalizations Service. The FBI also relied on the entire "US intelligence community", particularly the Central Intelligence Agency (CIA), the National Security Agency (NSA) and the Defense Intelligence Agency (DIA). Lastly, the FBI also benefited from international police cooperation, either from Interpol or directly through bilateral links with the police of allied states.

To collect clues, the FBI launched a call for witnesses on the evening of the attacks. In the course of the following three days, it received 3,800 telephone messages, 30,000 e-mails and 2,400 notifications from its intelligence agents.

The day after the attacks, the FBI had already managed to establish the *modus operandi* of the terrorists.[38] Agents of the bin Laden networks had entered American territory legally. Once inside the country, they had taken accelerated pilot training courses. Regrouped into four teams of five kamikazes each, they hijacked the airliners with the mission of crashing them into major objectives. On 14 September, the FBI published a list naming nineteen presumed plane hijackers.[39]

In the course of the following weeks, the international press reconstituted the life of the kamikazes. These reports showed that they did nothing to raise the suspicions of their friends and neighbors, or to allow Western police forces to take notice of them. Faded away into the general population, careful to avoid revealing their convictions, these "sleepers" would not be "woken" until the day of their mission. Other "sleeper agents", hidden in the shadows, were probably still waiting for their hour. An undetectable threat hovered over Western civilization...

* * *

On a methodological level, this was a visibly botched investigation. In criminal proceedings involving facts as complicated as these, the police should have constructed a number of hypotheses and followed each trail to the end, without neglecting any of them. The hypothesis of domestic terrorism was rejected in principle, without ever being studied. Instead, the finger was already being pointed at Osama bin Laden by *"sources close to the investigation"*, a few hours after the attacks. Public opinion demanded the guilty parties, so they were designated forthwith.

In each of the four hijacked planes, the terrorists were organized in teams of five men, brought together at the last moment. Nevertheless, there were only four terrorists on flight 93 that exploded over Pennsylvania: the fifth member of the commando team, Zacarias Moussaoui, was apprehended shortly before the attacks, due to his lack of a resident's card. Initially, the FBI claimed that all of the hijackers had been trained to sacrifice themselves. Later, after the discovery of a video cassette of Osama bin Laden, it was asserted that only the hijacker pirates were kamikazes, while their team-mates were informed at the last moment of the suicidal nature of their mission. Be that as it may, the idea of teams of kamikazes is a surprising one. The psychology of suicide is highly individual. During the Second World War, the Japanese kamikazes acted individually, even if their actions were coordinated in waves. More recently, the members of the Japanese Red Army (*Rengo Segikun*), who exported their technique to the Near East for the attack on Lodd (Israel, May 1972), acted in teams of three, but only after having had special training to weld themselves together as a unit. Even so, one of the Lodd terrorists, Kozo Okamoto, was captured alive. We don't know of any examples of kamikaze teams formed at the last minute.

Moreover, as Salman Rushdie mischievously pointed out[40], one can affirm that if the hijackers were in fact kamikazes, then they weren't Islamic fundamentalists. Indeed, the Koran forbids suicide. Fundamentalists (such as the Taliban, the Wahhabites and others) may expose themselves to death, as martyrs, without any hope of escape, but they wouldn't take their own lives.

Nevertheless, the kamikaze theory was confirmed by handwritten documents in Arabic which the FBI published in English translation and were reproduced by the international press.[41] Three copies were said to have been found: one in a suitcase that was lost in transit between flights, belonging to Mohammed Atta; the second in a vehicle abandoned at Dulles Airport by Nawaf Al-Hazmi and the third among the debris of flight 93 which exploded over Stony Creek Township, Pennsylvania.[42]

It contains four pages of pious advice:

"1) Recite the pledge you have taken to die and renew your intention. Shave your body and anoint it with eau de Cologne. Take a shower.

2) Make sure you are completely familiar with all the details of the plan and prepare yourself for an eventual riposte or reaction from the enemy.

3) Read Al-Tawba and Anfal [martial suras or chapters from the Koran], *reflect on their meaning and think of all that God has promised to martyrs."*

Etc.

Written in a classic theological style, often full of medieval references, these documents greatly contributed to feeding the image of fanatics that the American authorities exposed to popular wrath. Nevertheless, they were crude forgeries, whose incongruities would have been spotted by any person knowledgeable about Islam. For instance, they begin with the exhortation, *"In the name of God, of myself and of my family"* (sic), whereas Muslims – as opposed to numerous puritan sects in America – never pray in their own name, or that of their family.[43] Similarly, the text includes in one phrase an Americanism which has no place in vocabulary derived from the Koran: *"You must face it and understand it 100%"*

The FBI presented Mohammed Atta as the leader of the operation. In ten years, this 33 year old was said to have stayed in Salou (Spain), then Zurich (Switzerland) – where, according to investigators, he paid by credit card for Swiss knives destined to be used in the plane hijackings – and finally Hamburg (Germany). Along with two other terrorists, he took courses there in electronics, without causing comment about himself or letting his extremist convictions become known. Upon arriving in the United States, he joined his accomplices in Florida, took pilot courses in the town of Venice and even paid for several hours on a flight simulator in Miami. Anxious to disguise his fundamentalism, Mohammed Atta went as far as to frequent the Olympic Garden in Las Vegas, the biggest topless cabaret in the world. This peerless agent was believed to reached Boston on 11 September by a domestic flight. Given the short time between the two flights, he appears to have lost his baggage in transit. In searching them, the FBI found training videos on piloting Boeing aircraft, a book of Islamic prayers and an old letter in which he announces his intention to die as a martyr. Atta was identified as the head of the commando team by a steward who made a call with his cellular telephone during the hijacking and indicated the leader's seat number: 8D.

Should we take such information seriously? One would have to accept that Mohammed Atta spent ten years carefully hiding his real intentions and that he must have adhered to strict procedures in communicating with his accomplices to escape the attention of the intelligence services. Nevertheless, at the last moment he left behind a bagful of clues. Although he was the leader of the operation, he took the risk of missing his flight connection on September 11 and finally succeeded in joining American Airlines flight 11, but without recovering his baggage. But really, why burden yourself with baggage at all if you were about to commit suicide?

Even more ridiculous, the FBI claims to have discovered Mohammed Atta's passport intact in the smoking ruins of the World Trade Center! It's a true miracle; one wonders how this document could even have "survived" such an ordeal.

It's obvious that the FBI has presented pieces of evidence that it fabricated itself. Perhaps we should only see this as the panicked reaction of a police agency which had already demonstrated its incapacity to prevent the catastrophe and was trying by all means to restore its reputation.

More worrying is the controversy surrounding the identification of the kamikazes. The international press commented at length on the profiles of the nineteen terrorists designated by the FBI. All of them were men between twenty-five and thirty-five years old. They were Arabs and Muslims, for the most part from Saudi Arabia. They were well-educated. They were acting out of idealism rather than despair.

The only problem with these identikit portraits is that they are based on a list which itself is subject to dispute. The Saudi embassy in Washington has confirmed that Abdulaziz Al-Omari, Mohand Al-Shehri, Salem Al-Hazmi and Saeed Al-Ghamdi are all alive and well, and living in their own country. Waleed M. Al-Shehri, who lives at present in Casablanca and works as a pilot for Royal Air Maroc, gave an interview to the Arab-language daily, *Al-Qods al-Arabi*, based in London. Prince Saud Al-Faisal, the Saudi Foreign Minister, declared to the press that, *"It has been proven that five of the persons named in the FBI's list had no connection with what happened.*" And Prince Nayef, the Saudi Minister of the Interior, declared to an official American delegation, "*Until now, we have no evidence that assures us that they are related to September 11. We have not received anything in this regard from the United States.*"[44]

How were the terrorists identified? If one refers to the list of victims published by the airline companies on September 13, one is surprised not to see among them the names of the hijackers. It would seem that the criminals were removed in order to leave only "innocent victims" and crew members. If one counts the passengers, one finds 78 innocent victims on American Airlines flight 11 (which crashed into the north tower of the WTC), 46 on United Airlines flight 77 (which crashed into the south tower), 51 on American Airlines flight 77 (the one that supposedly crashed into the Pentagon) and 36 aboard United Airlines flight 93 (which exploded over Pennsylvania). These lists are incomplete, as several passengers were not identified.

If one refers to the press releases[45] issued by the airlines on September 11, one notes that flight 11 transported 81 passengers, flight 175 carried 56 passengers, flight 77 transported 58 passengers and flight 93 had 38 passengers.

It is thus physically impossible that flight 11 could have transported more than three terrorists and flight 93 more than two. The absence of the names of the hijackers on the passenger lists therefore does not mean they were withdrawn in order to remain "politically correct", but simply they were not to be found among the rest. Goodbye to the identification of Mohammed Atta by a steward, thanks to the seat number, 8D.

* * *

  To sum things up, the FBI invented a list of hijackers from which it drew an identikit portrait of the enemies of the West. We are asked to believe that these hijackers were Arab Islamic militants who were acting as kamikazes. The domestic American leads were dismissed. In reality, we know nothing, neither the identity of the "terrorists" nor their operational method. All hypotheses remain open. As in all criminal affairs, the first question that should be asked is, "Who profits from the crime?".

Concerning that precise subject, in the period following the attacks it was found that maneuvers characteristic of "insider trading" had taken place in the six days preceding September 11.[46] The stock of United Airlines (owner of the planes that crashed into the south tower of the World Trade Center and near Pittsburgh) fell artificially by 42%. In the case of American Airlines (owner of the plan that crashed into the north tower of the WTC and of the one that was said to have crashed into the Pentagon), its stock fell by 39%. No other airline companies in the world were the object of comparable maneuvers, with the exception of KLM Royal Dutch Airlines. From this, one can deduce that a plane belong to the Dutch company may have been chosen as the target for a fifth hijacking.

Similar movements were noted concerning sales (or "put") options of stock in Morgan Stanley Dean Witter & Co. which multiplied twelve-fold in the week preceding the attacks. This particular firm just happened to occupy 22 floors in the World Trade Center. The same thing occurred with the world's leading stockbrokers, Merrill Lynch & Co., whose headquarters is located in a neighboring building threatened with collapse, for which put options multiplied by a factor of twenty-five. And above all, this happened with put options for the insurance companies involved: Munich Re, Swiss Re and AXA.

The Securities & Exchange Commission of Chicago was the first to raise the alert. It noticed that on the Chicago stock exchange, insiders had made capital gains of 5 million dollars on United Airlines, 4 million dollars on stock in American Airlines, 1.2 million dollars on Morgan Stanley Dean Winter & Co. and 5.5 million dollars on Merrill Lynch & Co.

Wary of investigators, the insiders prudently renounced collecting another 2.5 million dollars in gains on American Airlines that they hadn't had time to cash in before the alert took place.

The supervisory authorities in each of the world's big stock exchanges tracked down the gains made through this insider trading. Investigations were coordinated by the International Organization of Securities Commissions (IOSCO).[47] On 15 October, it held a video-conference where the national authorities presented their interim reports. It appeared that the illicit gains added up to several hundred million dollars, constituting the "biggest case of insider trading ever committed".

Osama bin Laden, whose bank accounts have been blocked since 1998, does not dispose of the money needed for this speculative operation. The Taliban government of the Islamic Emirate of Afghanistan also lacks the financial means for this.

Indeed, President Bill Clinton ordered the freezing of all of the financial assets of O. bin Laden, his associates, and their associations and companies, by Executive Order 13099, signed symbolically on 7 August 1998 (the day of the American riposte to the bombings in Nairobi and Dar-es-Salaam. This decision was internationalized by U.N. Security Council Resolution 1193 (13 August 1998). Bill Clinton extended the measure to the bank accounts of the Taliban, and their associates and satellites, by Executive Order 13129 on 4 July 1999. Finally, the worldwide freeze of assets belonging to persons and organizations linked to the finance of "international terrorism" was pronounced by Resolution 1269 of the U.N. Security Council (19 October 1999). From that date onwards, it became rather ridiculous to continue speaking of the "millionaire O. bin Laden" since he no longer has any possible means of access to his personal fortune. The means at his disposal can only come from secret aid – state-sponsored or not –, which can no longer be that of the Islamic Emirate of Afghanistan.

It has been possible to establish that the greater part of the transactions were "handled" by the Deutsche Bank and its American investment subsidiary, Alex. Brown.[48] This company was directed until 1998 by a colorful figure, A.B. Krongard. A former captain in the Marines and an enthusiast of firearms and martial arts, this banker became an advisor to the director of the CIA, and since March 26, 2001, the official number three in the hierarchy of the American intelligence agency. Given the importance of the investigation and the influence of A.B. Krongard, one would have thought that Alex. Brown would have cooperated readily with the authorities to facilitate the identification of inside traders. But this was not the case.

Strangely indeed, the FBI gave up on exploring this line of inquiry and IOSCO closed its investigation without resolving the affair. It would nevertheless be easy to trace the capital movements because all of the bank-to-bank transactions are archived with two clearing organizations.[49] One could accept that, given the importance of what was at stake, that it would be possible to break banking secrecy and determine just who the happy beneficiaries of the 11 September attacks actually were. But nothing came of all this.[50]

* * *

Given the unprecedented means of investigation at its disposal, the FBI should have devoted itself to elucidating each of the contradictions that we have raised. It should have given priority to studying the message sent by the attackers to the Secret Service in order to identify them. It should have established what really happened at the Pentagon. It should have tracked down the insider financial dealers. It should have discovered the source of the messages sent to Odigo warning occupants of the World Trade Center two hours before the attacks took place. Etc.

Instead, as we have seen, far from conducting a criminal investigation, the FBI has applied itself to making clues disappear and silencing testimony. It has supported the version of a foreign attack and tried to strengthen its credibility by divulging an improvised list of the hijackers and fabricating false evidence (Mohammed Atta's passport, instructions to the kamikazes, etc.).

This manipulative operation was orchestrated by its director, Robert Mueller III, a key Bush appointee who coincidently took office the week before September 11.

Was this pseudo-investigation conducted to prepare for an equitable trial, or was it rather meant to hide from view domestic American culpability and justify the military operations to follow?

PART II

THE DEATH OF DEMOCRACY IN AMERICA

Chapter 5

RIPOSTE OR GODSEND?

On the evening of September 11, President Geor-ge W. Bush addressed the nation in a solemn televised message with mystical overtones[51]: *America was targe-ted for attack because we're the brightest beacon for freedom and opportunity in the world. And no one will keep that light from shining. Today, our nation saw Evil, the very worst of human nature. And we responded with the best of America — with the daring of our rescue wor-kers, with the caring for strangers and neighbors who came to give blood and help in any way they couldd [...] The search is underway for those who are behind these evil acts. I've directed the full resources of our intelli-gence and law enforcement communities to find those responsible and to bring them to justice. We will make no distinction between the terrorists who committed these acts and those who harbor them. Tonight, I ask for your prayers for all those who grieve, for the children whose worlds have been shattered, for all whose sense of safe-ty and security has been threatened. And I pray they will be comforted by a power greater than any of us, spoken through the ages in Psalm 23:* 'Even though I walk through the valley of the shadow of death, I fear no evil, for You are with me.' *This is a day when all Americans from every walk of life unite in our resolve for justice and peace. America has stood down enemies before, and we will do so this time. None of us will ever forget this day. Yet, we go forward to defend freedom and all that is good and just in our world. Thank you. Good night, and God bless America."*

Despite this message of unity, and at a moment when the responsibility of Osama bin Laden was still officially considered to be only a hypothesis, two contradictory political options were being advocated within his administration. The moderates, grouped around the Secretary of State, General Colin Powell and the outgoing Chairman of the Joint Chiefs of Staff, General Hugh Shelton, recommended a proportionate riposte, along the lines of that ordered by Bill Clinton in 1998. That year, Tomahawk missiles were fired, from submarines cruising in the Sea of Oman, at Al-Qaeda's training camps in Afghanistan and at the Al-Shifa laboratory in Sudan, in response to the attacks perpetrated against the United States embassies in Dar-es-Salaam and Nairobi. Against them, the "hawks" noted that those strikes had had no effect since Al-Qaeda had recommenced its attacks. According to this group, only military intervention on the ground in Afghanistan would permit the definitive eradication of Osama bin Laden's bases. But the campaign should not stop there, rather it should continue by destroying in a similar fashion all other potential threats, i.e. all those organizations and states liable to become a menace comparable to Afghanistan.

The aging Henry Kissinger[52], former Secretary of State and supervisor of all the clandestine operations carried out by the American secret services from 1969 to

1976, is the tutelary figure and source of inspiration for the hawks. The President's televised speech had barely ended[53] when Kissinger published an opinion piece on the *Washington Post*'s Internet site. He did not mince his words: *"The government should be charged with a systematic response that, one hopes, will end the way that the attack on Pearl Harbor ended – with the destruction of the system that is responsible for it. That system is a network of terrorist organizations sheltered in capitals of certain countries. In many cases we do not penalize those countries for sheltering the organizations; in other cases, we maintain something close to normal relations with them. [...] We do not yet know whether Osama bin Laden did this, although it appears to have the earmarks of a bin Laden-type operation. But any government that shelters groups capable of this kind of attack, whether or not they can be shown to have been involved in this attack, must pay an exorbitant price.[...] It is something we should do calmly, carefully and inexorably."*

* * *

While American public opinion remained in a state of shock and mourned its dead, the days of 12 and 13 September were dominated, within the U.S. administration and foreign ministries throughout the world, by three questions: Would George W. Bush designate Al-Qaeda as the party responsible for the attacks? What type of operation would he order in Afghanistan? And would he commit his country to a long term war against all his real and supposed enemies?

American officials multiplied leaks to the media pointing the finger at Osama bin Laden and his organization, Al-Qaeda, as both the masterminds and the material authors of the attacks. The CIA director, George Tenet, presented President Bush with a series of reports with intercepts of Al-Qaeda's communications on September 11.[54] The attacks were said to have been planned since two years earlier, and would be the beginning of a long series. Both the Capitol and the White House were among the targets. The leaders of Al-Qaeda mistakenly believed they had hit several targets. Thus they had *"thanked God for the explosions in the Capitol building"*, they praised the *"destruction of the White House"* and celebrated *"the Doctor's plan"* (i.e. Dr. Ayman Zawahri, the right-hand man of Osama bin Laden). The operation had been set in motion by Abu Zubayda, already suspected of being the organizer of the attack against the destroyer *USS Cole* in October 2000, who gave the signal that *"zero hour"* was at hand.

President Bush then addressed the press[55]:

"I have just completed a meeting with my national security team, and we have received the latest intelligence updates.

The deliberate and deadly attacks which were carried out yesterday against our country were more than acts of terror. They were acts of war. This will require our country to unite in steadfast determination and resolve. Freedom and democracy are under attack.

The American people need to know that we're facing a different enemy than we have ever faced. This enemy hides in shadows, and has no regard for human life. This is an enemy who preys on innocent and unsus-

pecting people, then runs for cover. But it won't be able to run for cover forever. This is an enemy that tries to hide. But it won't be able to hide forever. This is an enemy that thinks its harbors are safe. But they won't be safe forever.

This enemy attacked not just our people, but all freedom-loving people everywhere in the world. The United States of America will use all our resources to conquer this enemy. We will rally the world. We will be patient, we will be focused, and we will be steadfast in our determination.

This battle will take time and resolve. But make no mistake about it: we will win. [...] But we will not allow this enemy to win the war by changing our way of life or restricting our freedoms. This morning, I am sending to Congress a request for emergency funding authority, so that we are prepared to spend whatever it takes to rescue victims, to help the citizens of New York City and Washington, D.C. respond to this tragedy, and to protect our national security.

I want to thank the members of Congress for their unity and support. America is united. The freedom-loving nations of the world stand by our side. This will be a monumental struggle of Good versus Evil. But Good will prevail."

With the exception of the British Foreign Office which issued martial declarations, the world's foreign ministries observed President Bush's reactions with anxiety. They soon learned the German, Egyptian, French, Israeli and Russian intelligence services had all alerted in vain their American counterparts as to what was being prepared, the CIA having minimized the threat. They also wondered about the reliability of reports – suddenly quite voluble – from the CIA, and about the progress – too rapid – of the FBI's investigation. They feared that, in order to reassure domestic public opinion, President Bush would hastily designate a convenient culprit and commit his country to an immediate and disproportionate military riposte.

The same day, the United Nation's Security Council adopted its Resolution 1368.[56] It recognized *"the inherent right* [of the United States] *to individual or collective self-defense in accordance with the Charter"* [of San Francisco]. It stipulated that the Security Council *"calls on all States to work together urgently to bring to justice the perpetrators, organizers and sponsors of these terrorist attacks and stresses that those responsible for aiding, supporting or harboring the perpetrators, organizers and sponsors of these acts will be held accountable."* In other words, the Security Council recognized the right of the United States to violate if necessary the sovereignty of states that protect the authors of the attacks, to arrest these terrorists and then bring them before an international court of justice. It did not, however, authorize the U.S. to pass justice themselves or attack states and overthrow their governments.

In the evening, the Council of the North Atlantic Treaty Organization (NATO) met behind closed doors. The member states decided to lend assistance to the United States – but not to commit their own forces – in its response to the attack of which they had been victim. The Council was unusually tense. Certain members thought that attacks could have been ordered from within the American state apparatus and refused to commit themselves to a *"war on terrorism"* whose objectives and limits were badly defined. As he left the meeting, NATO's secretary-general, Lord George Robertson, declared: *"If it is determined that this attack was directed from abroad against the United States, it shall be regarded as an action covered by Article 5 of the Washington Treaty"*[57] Worried by the turn of events, French President Jacques Chirac went to the United States for a visit which had already been scheduled for some time. On the one hand, he made numerous declaration expressing a warm solidarity with the American people. On the other, he organized a joint press conference with the Secretary-General of the United Nations, Kofi Annan, which sought to cool the United State's overheated reaction. *"The American riposte must be brought to bear on identified terrorists and possibly on those countries or groups for which we have proof that they supplied aid to these identified terrorist groups"*.[58]

The fear in diplomatic circles seemed be confirmed by an incident that occurred during a joint press conference[59] by the Attorney General, John Ashcroft, and the FBI director, Robert Mueller III. The chief of the federal police was explaining to reporters the need not to hurry the investigation that would gather the necessary proof to convict suspects, when the head of the Justice Department brutally interrupted him. John Ashcroft emphasized that time pressed and that the FBI's mission was to round up as quickly as possible the terrorists' accomplices before they committed other crimes. So much for gathering evidence.

On 13 September, the official tone sharpened. In the morning, the White House was partially evacuated following an anti-terrorist alert – it was becoming a habit – and Vice President Cheney was sent to a distant secure location. It was a false alert but a real psychodrama. In the afternoon, it was the Deputy Defense Secretary, Paul Wolfowitz, who presented the Pentagon's press briefing.[60] Wolfowitz was the widely recognized spokesman of the most extreme conservative group within the military-industrial lobby. For years he had militated in favor of *"finishing the dirty work"* in Iraq and saw in the events of September 11 an easy justification for the desired overthrow of Saddam Hussein. He did not cite any target during the press conference, neither Afghanistan nor Iraq. But he emphasized that the American response would be *"a campaign, not an isolated action"*. And he insisted:

"We're going to keep after these people and the people who support them until this stops. And it has to be treated that way."

Thinking that he might cut some ground from under the feet of the hawkish faction, the Secretary of State, Colin Powell, presented O. bin Laden as *"the principal suspect"* and prepared rapidly for an intervention – which he wished to be limited – in Afghanistan. He addressed a sort of ultimatum to Pakistan, calling upon it to place all its military infrastructure at the United States' disposal and to immediately cut off all political and economic ties with the Taliban regime.[61]

* * *

In reality, as we shall see, the debate that agitated Washington was by no means new. The two options (strikes on Afghanistan or a generalized war on terrorism) had been studied and prepared before the attacks. Their rationales were not linked to the events of September 11, even if the latter provided a pretext for going ahead. Consequently, the quarrel revolved around whether public opinion would accept only targeted strikes, or if it was sufficiently shocked to allow for a prolonged war. In the end, the psychological blow turned out to be so great that strategists in Washington were not forced to choose and could activate both options.

In mid-July 2001, taking note of the failure of multi-party negotiations in Berlin on the future of Afghanistan, the American delegation led by Tom Simmons (former ambassador to Pakistan), Karl Inderfurth (former assistant to the Secretary of State) and Lee Coldren (former expert at the State Department) adopted a threatening attitude. According to the former Pakistani ambassador to Paris, Niaz Naik, who took part in the talks, the Americans declared that they would invade Afghanistan in mid-October and overthrow the Taliban regime.[62]

At the beginning of September, under the cover of its annual maneuvers in the Sea of Oman, *Essential Harvest*, the United Kingdom proceeded with one of most important fleet deployments since the Falklands War and amassed its troops off the shores of Pakistan, while NATO transported 40,000 troops to the region to take part in the *Bright Star* maneuvers in Egypt. Thus, the Anglo-American forces were already pre-positioned in the zone before the attacks took place.

As for the "*war on terrorism*", the United States military planners had been preparing it in some detail through two major war games: Global Engagement IV and JEFX 99.[63] The tactical procedures were worked out in a final simulation in June 2000. But the war game initially scheduled for June 2001 was cancelled, which the officers concerned interpreted as a sign that the real thing was imminent.

The United States has always been reluctant to take the initiative in war. In the past, they took pains to present their military engagements as legitimate ripostes. With the attacks of September 11, they found an opportunity they had been dreaming for.

Chapter 6

FROM THE FUNERAL PRAYERS
TO HOLY WAR

Since one rarely wages war without putting God on one's side, it was more often American preachers rather than military strategists that one found invading the television studios after September 11. All of them interpreted the attacks as a divine sign calling America to convert. "*God Almighty has withdrawn his protection from us*", wrote the Reverend Pat Robertson, leader of the highly influential Christian Coalition, "*because we wallow in the search for material pleasures and sex*".

Pastor Robertson received his friend Pastor Jerry Falwell on his star program, *700 Club* (Fox Channel). The two TV evangelists analyzed the events that had just plunged America into mourning.[64] "*God continues to lift the curtain and allow the enemies of America to give us what we probably deserve*", Falwell declared. "*Jerry, that's my feeling,*" Robertson replied. "*I think we've just seen the antechamber to terror. We haven't even begun to see what they can do to the major population.*"

Falwell then blamed the American Civil Liberties Union (ACLU), the federal courts, and all those who were "*throwing God out of the public square.*" "*The abortionists have got to bear some burden for this because God will not be mocked,"* he continued. *"And when we destroy 40 million little innocent babies, we make God mad. I really believe that the pagans, and the abortionists, and the feminists, and the gays and the lesbians who are actively trying to make that an alternative lifestyle, the ACLU, People for the American Way – all of them who have tried to secularize America – I point the finger in their face and say,* 'You helped this happen'."

It is in this context – where religious rhetoric serves political and military interests – that, taking on the role of spiritual chief of America and the civilized world, President Bush issued the following decree[65]:

"All our hearts have been seared by the sudden and sense-less taking of innocent lives. We pray for healing and for the strength to serve and encourage one another in hope and faith. Scripture says: 'Blessed are those who mourn for they shall be comforted.' *I call on every American family and the family of America to observe a National Day of Prayer and Remembrance, honoring the memory of the thousands of victims of these brutal attacks and comforting those who lost loved ones. We will persevere through this national tragedy and personal loss. In time, we will find healing and recovery; and, in the face of all this evil, we remain strong and united,* 'one Nation under God'.

NOW, THEREFORE, I, GEORGE W. BUSH, President of the United States of America, by virtue of the authority vested in me by the Constitution and laws of the United States, do hereby proclaim Friday, September 14, 2001, as a National Day of Prayer and Remembrance for the Victims of the Terrorist Attacks on September

11, 2001. I ask that the people of the United States and places of worship mark this National Day of Prayer and Remembrance with noontime memorial services, the ringing of bells at that hour, and evening candlelight remembrance vigils. I encourage employers to permit their workers time off during the lunch hour to attend the noontime services to pray for our land. I invite the people of the world who share our grief to join us in these solemn observances.

IN WITNESS WHEREOF, I have hereunto set my hand this thirteenth day of September, in the year of our Lord two thousand one, and of the Independence of the United States of America the two hundred and twenty-sixth."[66]

An unprecedented ceremony took place in the National Cathedral. President and Mrs. Bush, four former Presidents (Bill Clinton, George Bush Sr., Jimmy Carter and Gerald Ford) and nearly all of Congress came together in prayer. A cardinal, a rabbi and an imam all took turns in leading the proceedings. The most famous TV evangelist in the world, Pastor Billy Graham, who had converted George W. Bush fifteen years earlier, pronounced a homily[67]: "*One of the things we desperately need is a spiritual renewal in this country. We need a spiritual revival in America. And God has told us in His Word, time after time, that we are to repent of our sins and we're to turn to Him and He will bless us in a new way. [...] But now we have a choice: whether to implode and disintegrate emotionally and spiritually as a people and a nation — or, whether we choose to become stronger through all of this struggle — to rebuild on a solid foundation. And I believe that we are in the process of starting to rebuild on that foundation. That foundation is our trust in God. . [...] We also know that God is going to give wisdom and courage and strength to the President and those around him. And this is going to be a day that we will remember as a day of victory."*

President Bush then mounted to the pulpit and also delivered a sermon.[68] It had been prepared by his adviser, the fundamentalist Biblical scholar Michael Gearson: " [...] *Our responsibility to history is already clear: to answer these attacks and rid the world of Evil. War has been waged against us by stealth and deceit and murder. This nation is peaceful, but fierce when stirred to anger [...] God's signs are not always the ones we look for. We learn in tragedy that his purposes are not always our own. Yet the prayers of private suffering, whether in our homes or in this great cathedral, are known and heard, and understood. There are prayers that help us last through the day, or endure the night. There are prayers of friends and strangers, that give us strength for the journey. And there are prayers that yield our will to a will greater than our own [...] America is a nation full of good fortune, with so much to be grateful for. But we are not spared from suffering. In every generation, the world has produced enemies of human freedom. They have attacked America, because we are freedom's home and defender. And the commitment of our fathers is now the calling of our time. On this national day of prayer and remembrance, we ask almighty God to watch over our nation, and grant us patience and resolve in all that is to come. We pray that He will comfort and console those who now walk in sorrow. We thank Him for each life we now must mourn, and the promise of a life to come. As we have been assured, neither death nor life, nor angels nor principalities nor powers, nor things pre-*

sent nor things to come, nor height nor depth, can sepa-
rate us from God's love. May He bless the souls of the
departed. May He comfort our own. And may He always
guide our country. God bless America."

The *Washington Post* would later analyze the metamorphosis of George W. Bush:

"For the first time since religious conservatives
became a modern political movement, the president of the
United States has become the movement's de facto leader
– a status even Ronald Reagan, though admired by reli-
gious conservatives, never earned. Christian publications,
radio and television shows shower Bush with praise, while
preachers from the pulpit treat his leadership as an act of
providence. A procession of religious leaders who have
met with him testify to his faith, while Web sites encoura-
ge people to fast and pray for the president."[69]

At noon on 14 September, following the prayer by the President of the United States, the 43 states of the Council of Europe[70] (including Russia) and many other countries on all continents, observed three minutes of silence in memory of the victim of the attacks. All of them thus tacitly accepted the leadership of a fundamentalist born-again Christian who had announced his intention to lead them into a *"monumental struggle of Good versus Evil"*.[71] Were the political-cum-mystical ravings of the television evangelists contagious?

Neither the psychological shock, nor the respect that one might feel for the deceased, can explain this intense religious fervor. If the United States were originally a theocracy founded by Puritans fleeing the intolerance of the British Crown, they were by no means this overly devout nation where the TV evangelists had taken on the role of military strategists. There was moreover

no historical precedent of an American president pro-
nouncing a declaration of war in a cathedral.

George W. Bush's call to the *"peoples of the world
who share our suffering to join these solemn observances*
[of religious ceremonies]" was complied with even in the
secular French republic. Thus, both French heads of the
executive, President Jacques Chirac and Prime Minister
Lionel Jospin, signed on 12 September a decree worded
in the following manner: *"Friday, 14 September 2001 is
declared a national day of mourning in homage to the
victims of the attacks committed in the United States of
America on 11 September 2001"*.[72] Accompanied by a
throng of elected officials and ministers, they had gone
the night before to an ecumenical service at the American
Church in Paris, where together, they had intoned the
famous hymn, *God Bless America!*

These prayers imposed by decree raised, here and
there, some lively controversy. Opponents pointed out
that this worldwide hand-wringing seemed to imply that
the thousands of American victims were somehow worth
more than all the victims of recent genocides, none of
whom received such honors. We should try to understand
this controversy as a refusal to accept political manipulation of religious sentiment. Three minutes of silence to
foster awareness that conflicts can be resolved peaceful-
ly, without recourse to terrorism, might have been uni-
versally accepted, but not a prayer solely for the victims
of terrorism on American territory. These ceremonies did
not express a collective aspiration for peace, but sought
to justify future vengeance.

This moment of prayer constituted a historical
turning point. The United States went to war as the
national anthem rang out in the cathedral, the *Washing-*

ton Post write later.[73] A statement that could be extended: the world went to war by associating itself with America's mourning.

In that light, we should ask ourselves why this unanimous homage was organized. Unlike the mobilization of military alliances, no international treaty stipulates the obligation to gather together in prayer when the United States are in mourning. It was nevertheless easier and faster to decree international mourning than to bring into play the NATO, ANZUS and OAS treaties.[74] Looking more closely, one notes that the French decree was signed by Jacques Chirac and Lionel Jospin on 12 September, i.e., before George W. Bush even proclaimed the American day of mourning. Such an operation on a planetary scale required the activation of a network of influence capable of applying pressure on nearly every government in the world. Above all, this operation had a political goal: by manipulating religious sentiment, the American government consecrated not only the victims of the attacks, but also its version of events. From then on, any questioning of the official truth would be seen as sacrilege.

The arrangements used to impose international mourning were secretly given a more formal basis in October 2001.[75] The Office for Strategic Influence[76] was created at the Pentagon and placed under General Simon Pete Worden, former head of the U.S. Space Command. This body was connected with the International Information Programs[77] at the State Department – which includes the broadcasts of Voice of America radio – via the International Military Information Group directed by Colonel Brad Ward. It now works flat out to manipulate Western public opinion and Western governments.[78]

Chapter 7

EMERGENCY POWERS

On the morning of 14 September the United States Congress authorized President George W. Bush to resort to *"all necessary and appropriate force against those nations, organizations or persons he determines planned, authorized, committed or aided the terrorist attacks that occurred on September 11, 2001, or harbored such organizations or persons, in order to prevent any future acts of international terrorism against the United States by such nations, organizations or persons."*[79]

This joint resolution of both houses was adopted unanimously minus one vote, that of the Democratic Representative from California, Barbara Lee[80], with almost no debate. Its wording gives full latitude to President Bush to combat non-governmental terrorist organizations, but the "emergency powers" granted are not quite "war powers". George W. Bush remains obliged to inform Congress before initiating hostilities against another state.[81]

In order to conduct the first operations, President Bush asked Congress for a special credit of twenty billion dollars. In an emotive surge of patriotic spirit, the two Houses doubled this amount and at the close of five hours of debate voted a credit of... forty billion dollars.[82]

In addition, President Bush authorized the mobilization of a maximum of fifty thousand reservists.[83] The Secretary of Defense, Donald Rumsfeld, called up 35,500 immediately (10,000 for the Army, 13,000 for the Air Force, 3,000 for the Navy, 7,500 for the Marines, and 2,000 for the Coast Guard). The last mobilization of this kind dates back to the Gulf War. The latter concerned five times as many troops, because then it entailed bringing together a powerful armada.

George W. Bush delivered an important speech[84] to Congress, meeting in joint session, on September 20. He was accompanied by numerous public figures, including the British Prime Minister, Tony Blair. On this occasion, he at last officially designated Osama bin Laden and his organization as responsible for the attacks and launched an ultimatum to the Taliban regime: *"Deliver to United States authorities all the leaders of Al-Qaeda who hide in your land. Release all foreign nationals, including American citizens, you have unjustly imprisoned. Protect foreign journalists, diplomats and aid workers in your country. Close immediately and permanently every terrorist training camp in Afghanistan, and hand over every terrorist, and every person in their support structure, to appropriate authorities. Give the United States full access to terrorist training camps, so we can make sure they are no longer operating. These demands are not open to negotiation or discussion. The Taliban must act, and act immediately. They will hand over the terrorists, or they will share in their fate."*

Beyond that, he announced the creation of a new Office of Homeland Security, with Cabinet rank and placed directly under his authority. This new body will *"develop and coordinate the implementation of a comprehensive national strategy to secure the United States from terrorist threats or attacks.*" The President added that he was appointing the former Marine and Governor of Pennsylvania, Tom Ridge, to direct this Office.

As a complement to these measures, the Bush Administration took several decisions to strengthen military secrecy.

As early as the day following the attacks, 12 September, Secretary Rumsfeld had declared during his press briefing at the Pentagon: "*It seems to me that it's important to underline that when people deal with intelligence information and make it available to people who are not cleared for that classified information, the effect is to reduce the chances that the United States government has to track down and deal with the people who have perpetrated the attacks on the United States and killed so many Americans. Second, when classified information dealing with operations is provided to people who are not cleared for that classified information, the inevitable effect is that the lives of men and women in uniform are put at risk because they are the ones who will be carrying out those prospective operations.*"[85]

Questioned by reporters, on September 25, as to whether he intended to lie in order to preserve secrets, Rumsfeld answered that, personally, he was clever enough to find other ways of maintaining secrecy, but that his collaborators would have to do the best they could:[86]

Secretary of Defense Rumsfeld: *Of course, this conjures up Winston Churchill's famous phrase when he said — don't quote me on this, okay? I don't want to be quoted on this, so don't quote me. He said sometimes the truth is so precious it must be accompanied by a bodyguard of lies — talking about the invasion date and the* *invasion location. And indeed, they engaged not just in not talking about the date of the Normandy invasion or the location, whether it was to be Normandy Beach or just north off of Belgium, they actually engaged in a plan to confuse the Germans as to where it would happen. And they had a fake army under General Patton and one thing and another thing. That is a piece of history, and I bring it up just for the sake of background. I don't recall that I've ever lied to the press, I don't intend to, and it seems to me that there will not be reason for it. There are dozens of ways to avoid having to put yourself in a position where you're lying. And I don't do it.*

Reporter: *That goes for everybody in the Department of Defense?*

Rumsfeld: *You've got to be kidding.* (Laughter.)

On October 2, the Under-Secretary of Defense, Pete Aldridge, Jr., addressed a letter to all military suppliers.[87] He indicated to them that military secrecy extended to their commercial activities, it being understood that even apparently anodyne information could reveal much about the activities and intentions of the Department of Defense. Discretion was thus necessary henceforth on the part of civilians.

An e-mail[88] was also sent on 4 October by the purchasing director of the U.S. Air Force, Darlene Druyun, to all suppliers to make clear the ramifications of Aldridge's letter. It prohibited all suppliers from discussing with journalists both contracts under negotiation and those that had already been signed and made public. The prohibition was valid not only within the United States but also in all foreign countries where suppliers participated in salons or colloquia on armaments.

On October 5, President Bush, in violation of the US Constitution, ordered several members of his Cabinet to cease transmitting information to members of Congress (see Documents & Appendices).

The Deputy Defense Secretary, Paul Wolfowitz, addressed a note on 18 October to the Department's bureau chiefs, for circulation to all personnel. He wrote: *"It is therefore vital that Defense Department employees, as well as persons in other organizations that support DoD, exercise* great *caution in discussing information related to DoD work, regardless of their duties. Do not conduct* any *work-related conversations in common areas, public places, while commuting, or over unsecured electronic circuits. Classified information may be discussed* only *in authorized spaces and with persons having a specific need to know and the proper security clearance. Unclassified information may likewise require protection because it can often be compiled to reveal sensitive conclusions. Much of the information we use to conduct DoD's operations must be withheld from public release because of its sensitivity. If in doubt, do not release or discuss official information with other DoD personnel."*

At the same time, the federal authorities were taking measures to guarantee the secrecy of the investigation into the attacks. On September 11, the FBI asked the airlines not to communicate with the press. Yet their testimony would help elucidate both the reasons why the planes were not filled, and why the hijackers were not on the passenger lists. That very evening, the FBI were waiting at the home of brothers Jules and Gidéon Naudet who had been in Manhattan at the time of the crashes. The FBI confiscated five hours of video recordings, filmed by the two journalist in the interior of the WTC towers and on the platforms outside. Only six minutes of recordings, corresponding to the crash of the first plane, were returned to them. This document, which would permit a better understanding of the collapse of the World Trade Center, was placed under seals. The FBI also asked the Odigo company not to communicate with the press. It would be interesting, however, to know the exact content of the warning they received and the measures taken to limit the number of persons in the towers that day. Similarly, the military authorities forbade all contact between their personnel and the press. Journalists are thus unable to question either the fighter pilots or the personnel at Barksdale and Offutt Air Force bases. The American Bar Association, for its part, aware that trials for compensation and damages stemming from the attacks would provide opportunities to reveal official secrets, announced that it would remove from the bar any jurist who attempted to initiate legal proceedings in the name of victims' families. This prohibition was to last only for a period of six months, beyond which certain kinds of tests or appraisals are no longer possible.

President Bush personally contacted the leaders of Congress asking them not to endanger national security by creating a panel of inquiry into the events of September 11. As a matter of saving face, as well as turning the page, the Congressional leaders decided to create a joint inquiry from both Houses.. concerning measures taken since September 11 to prevent new terrorist attacks.[89]

On October 10, the National Security adviser, Condoleezza Rice, called to the White House the directors of the major television networks (ABC, CBS, CNN, Fox, Fox News, MSNBC and NBC) to appeal to their sense of responsibilities. If freedom of expression remained the rule, journalists were invited to exercise their own "editorial judgment" concerning information and to abstain from broadcasting anything that might be harmful to the security of the American people.[90]

The message was also received loud and clear by the written press. Immediately, Ron Gutting (editor-in-chief of the *City Sun*) and Dan Guthrie (editor-in-chief of the *Daily Courier*), who had dared to criticize the Bush line, were dismissed.

"*Pravda and* Isvestia *in the former Soviet Union would have been hard-pressed to surpass the American media in their subservience to the official agenda* [...] *They have abandoned the notion of objectivity or even the idea of providing a public space where problems are discussed and debated.* [...] *It's a scandal that reveals the existence of a system of propaganda, not of serious media so essential in a democratic society*", commented Edward Herman, Professor of Political Science at the University of Pennsylvania.[91]

Finally, at the end of three weeks of debates, Congress adopted the Uniting and Strengthening America by Providing Appropriate Tools Required to Intercept and Obstruct Terrorism Act (which gives us the acronym USA PATRIOT Act). This exceptional legislation suspends various civil liberties for a period of four years in order to give the United States government the means of fighting terrorism effectively. It escaped no one that four years covers the totality of George W. Bush's tenure in office, including the electoral period prior to a second mandate. It represses "*terrorists and those who support them*", according to a very extensive definition. Thus, the collection of funds to support the families of IRA members imprisoned in the United Kingdom has become a federal crime. The length of detention without charges being brought in the case of foreigners suspected of terrorism has been extended to a week. In case of charges being brought (for whatever cause, without any necessary link to suspicion of terrorism), the suspects may be held in secret for up to six months, renewable without limits if the Attorney General believes that their release *"endangers national security or that of society in general"*. Immediately, 1,200 immigrants were placed in detention for an indefinite period on undisclosed charges. Foreign consular agents have complained of infringements of the fundamental rights of citizens of their respective countries, as in the case of the Consul-General of Pakistan in New York, who declared: *"In most cases, we have neither the identity, nor the place of detention of our nationals. At best, we are given the numbers detained. The U.S. authorities are also putting pressure on them to prevent their exercise of their rights to contact consular representatives and lawyers. It's completely inadmissible."*

The USA PATRIOT Act lastly permits the FBI to intercept communications without supervision by a judge.[92]

On October 31, the Department of Justice suspended the right of persons placed in detention to converse alone with their legal counsel.[93] Henceforth, these meetings could be observed and recorded, and remarks could be used against the suspects, which eliminates any possibility for the client and his lawyer to elaborate a defense strategy together.

On 13 November, President Bush decreed that foreigners *"suspected of terrorism"*, including *"members and former members of Al-Qaeda"* and people having helped (even unknowingly) to conspire with a view to committing terrorist acts (even those not carried out) would not be judged by federal courts, nor even by military courts, but by new military commissions.[94] These will be appointed at the discretion of the Secretary of Defense and will establish their own Code of Procedure. Their sessions can held behind closed doors. The "military prosecutors" are not required to communicate to the accused or their defenders the "evidence" they may have at their disposal. The commissions' decisions will be reached by a two-thirds majority of their members (and not unanimously as is the international norm in criminal cases).

The same day, the Department of Justice arrested 5,000 suspects of Middle-Eastern extraction, practically all of them with their immigration status in order and without police records, for "questioning".

With the backing of the Counter-Terrorism Committee[95] created by Resolution 1373[96] (28 September 2001) of the U.N. Security Council, the State Department pressed its allies through the U.N. to adopt similar legislation. As of today, 55 countries (including France through its "law on day-to-day security") have thus transcribed into their domestic laws certain provisions of the USA PATRIOT Act. Their aim is not to protect local populations from terrorism, but to permit the U.S. police services to extend their activities to the rest of the world. They essentially entail lengthening the period of detention of suspects in terrorist cases, limiting freedom of the press, and authorizing the interception of communications without judicial controls. In the United Kingdom, the anti-terrorist law allows the detention of foreign suspects without judicial proceedings, in violation of the

European Declaration on Human Rights. In Canada, the anti-terrorist law requires journalists to reveal their sources upon order from a magistrate or risk immediate imprisonment. In Germany, the intelligence services have been granted judicial powers converting them into a veritable political police. The Italian secret services are authorized to commit all kinds of criminal acts on national territory, in the interest of national defense, without being accountable to the judiciary. Etc.[97]

Finally, the Secretary of State, Colin Powell, came to Europe seeking to ensure that national police forces would henceforth transmit information in their possession to the FBI without bureaucratic formalities, and allow the FBI to install a team in the offices of Europol.

* * *

"Since September 11, the government has enacted legislation, adopted policies, and threatened procedures that are not consistent with our established laws and values and would have been unthinkable before," wrote the prestigious *New York Review of Books*.[98] Glorifying in its patriotic mystique, the land of free expression and political transparency has fallen back on an extensive conception of *raison d'Etat* and military secrecy which is being applied to all sectors of society.

The official version of the events of September 11 do not justify such a sudden change. If the enemy are poor wretches hiding out in the caves of Afghanistan, why fear conversations between colleagues within the confines of the Pentagon? How is it conceivable that a handful of terrorists might be able to gather and treat scattered information on arms purchases and deduce from them the plans of the U.S. Army? Why suspend the normal functioning of institutions and deny members of Congress, even behind closed doors, information that is indispensable to democratic governance?

And if the official story, according to which the attacks were perpetrated by foreign terrorists, is true, why block any Congressional inquiry or any press investigation?

Are we not witness a change of political regime that was programmed well before September 11? On several occasions over the past half-century, the CIA has attempted to promote the adoption of legislation prohibiting the press from evoking affairs of state and criminalizing civil servants and journalists who reveal them. In November 2000, the extremely reactionary Senator Richard Shelby, who then chaired the Senate Intelligence Committee, instigated the passage of an Official Secrecy Act which was vetoed by President Bill Clinton. Richard Shelby repeated the maneuver in August 2001, hoping for a better welcome from President Bush.[99] The bill was under discussion when the September 11 attacks occurred, and parts of it were incorporated into the Intelligence Act of 13 December 2001. Immediately, Attorney General John Ashcroft created a special unit charged with evaluating means of preventing leaks of classified information.[100] It was to deliver a report in six months' time. But already, numerous official Web sites have been cleaned up: public information has been withdrawn on the grounds that its collation could permit "terrorists" to deduce secret information.

The judiciary, Congressional inquiries, and the press, i.e. all the countervailing powers, have been neutralized, while the executive branch has given itself new structures that will permit it to extend to domestic politics the methods already tested by the CIA and the military abroad.

The creation of the Office of Homeland Security (OHS), announced to Congress by President Bush on September 20, only came into effect on October 8. It is not a temporary measure dictated by circumstances, but a profound reform of the American state apparatus. Henceforth, the government will distinguish between domestic and external security. The director of the OHS (Tom Ridge) will be the equal of the National Security adviser (Condoleezza Rice). Each chairs a Council: the Council of Homeland Security and the National Security Council. Their respective competences overlap in numerous domains. Also, President Bush has appointed a Deputy National Security adviser to oversee the anti-terrorism effort, who, although reporting to Condoleezza Rice, should also be at the disposal of Tom Ridge. This key position was entrusted to General Wayne A. Downing, whose profile is particularly *"muscular"*.[101] Among other things, Downing was the head of the Special Operations Command for the *"stay-behind"* network.[102] He will also ensure cooperation between the two councils and the Office of Strategic Influence, charged with manipulating public opinion and governments abroad.

The Office of Homeland Security has vast powers of coordination that could evolve with time. It is difficult to say whether it will play a comparable role to that of the Office of War Mobilization (OWM) during the Second World War, or that of the Office of National Drug Control Policy (ONDCP) which supervises military operations in Latin America.[103] In any case, we are seeing a takeover of civilian life by the military and the intelligence agencies.[104]

"Historians will record that between November 2000 and February 2002, democracy — as envisioned by the creators of the Declaration of Independence and the U.S. Constitution — effectively came to an end. As democracy died, the Fascist American Theocratic State was born." commented two great journalists, John Stanton and Wayne Madsen.[105]

PART III

THE EMPIRE ATTACKS

Chapter 8

BIN LADEN'S TO BLAME!

On the morning of September 11, when CNN broadcast the first pictures of one of the World Trade Center towers on fire, but it was still not yet known whether it was an accident or the result of an attack, the commentators for the network raised the possibility that Osama bin Laden might be responsible. This hypothesis progressively imposed itself as the only humanly acceptable explanation. Attacks of such a barbarous nature could only be the work of a monster, radically foreign to the civilized world, filled with an irrational hatred of the West, and whose hands were covered in blood. This lunatic had already been identified: it was the United States' Public Enemy N°1, Osama bin Laden. The rumor was fed initially by leaks to the press from "*generally well-informed sources*" or "*sources close to the investigation*". It became official when Colon Powell publicly called bin Laden a "*suspect*". It became a dogma when George W. Bush named him as the guilty party. To this day, that accusation has not been publicly backed up by proof. But the American authorities believe themselves exempted from doing so by the publication of a video of Osama bin Laden which to their minds amounted to a confession.

Osama bin Laden[106] is one of fifty-four children of Sheikh Mohammed bin Laden, founder in 1931 of the Saudi Binladen Group (SBG). This holding, the most important in Saudi Arabia, derives about half of its revenues from construction and public works, and the other half from engineering, real estate, distribution, telecommunications and publishing. It formed a Swiss investment firm, the Saudi Investment Company (SICO), which created several companies in partnership with subsidiaries of the Saudi National Commercial Bank. The SBG has important holdings in General Electric, Nortel Networks and Cadbury Schweppes. It is represented in the United States by Adnan Kashoggi (the ex-brother-in-law of Mohammed Al-Fayed), while its financial assets are managed by the Carlyle Group. Up until 1996, the setting-up of the SBG's subsidiaries were prepared in Lausanne by its councilor, the Nazi banker François Genoud, executor of Dr. Goebbels's will and a donor of funds to the terrorist Carlos. The SBG is indissolubly linked to the Wahhabite regime in Saudi Arabia, to the point of having been for a long time the one and only contractor for the construction and management of the kingdom's holy places, Medina and Mecca. Similarly, it won the majority of building contracts for U.S. bases in Saudi Arabia and for the reconstruction of Kuwait after the Gulf War. After the accidental death of Sheik Mohammed bin Laden in 1968, his eldest son, Salem, succeeded him. He died in his turn in a plane "accident" that occurred in Texas, in 1988. Since then, the SBG has been directed by Bakr, the founder's second son.

Born in 1957, Osama received a diploma in management and economics from King Abdul Aziz University. He was reputed to be a prudent businessman. In December 1979, he was approached by his tutor, Prince Turki Al-Faisal Al-Saud (director of the Saudi secret services from 1977 to August 2001), to financially manage the CIA's secret operations in Afghanistan. Over a period of ten years, the CIA invested two billion dollars in Afghanistan to hold the Soviets in check, making these the most expensive operations in the agency's history. The Saudi and United States services recruited Islamic militants, trained them, armed them, and manipulated them in a *jihad* (holy war) to combat and defeat the Soviets for them.[107] Osama bin Laden managed the needs of this irregular milieu on a computer file called "*Al-Qaeda*" (literally, the "base", as in data base).

After the defeat of the USSR, the USA completely lost interest in the fate of Afghanistan, which they left in the hands of warlords and the *mujahiddin* they had recruited from throughout the Muslim world to fight the Red Army. Osama bin Laden supposedly then ceased to work for the CIA and recovered these fighters for his own purposes. In 1990, he is said to have proposed putting his men at the service of the Saudi monarchy to expel the lay apostate Saddam Hussein from Kuwait, and was angered when the Saudis preferred the coalition led by Bush senior (President), Dick Cheney (at that time Secretary of Defense) and Colin Powell (then Chairman of the Joint Chiefs of Staff).

The Islamic militants soon split into two camps, according to whether they were allies or adversaries of the Saudi-American coalition. O. bin Laden belonged to the faction headed by the Sudanese leader Hassan El-Tourabi, in which Yasser Arafat could also be found. They participated together in the Arab and Islamic Popular Conferences held in Khartoum.

In 1992, the United States debarked in Somalia,

under a UN mandate for the "Restore Hope" operation. A few veterans from Afghanistan opened fire against the GI's there. They participated in a operation during which eighteen American soldiers were killed. Osama bin Laden was designated as the party responsible for these skirmishes. The U.S. Army packed its bags and left. In the collective imagination, bin Laden had just defeated the Americans, after having beaten the Soviets.

Osama bin Laden was at that point stripped of his Saudi nationality and installed himself in Sudan. In breaking with his family, he received an inheritance estimated at 300 million dollars.[108] He invested these funds in the creation of several banks, agricultural businesses, and local distributors. At first with the support of Colonel Omar Hassan El-Bechir, then Hassan El-Tourabi, he developed various companies in Sudan, building an airport and roads, installing a pipeline and controlling the major part of the production of gum-arabic. Despite these projects, he was expelled from Sudan in 1996, after pressure from Egypt, which accused him of fomenting a assassination attempt on President Hosni Mubarak. He then returned to Afghanistan.

In June 1996, nineteen American soldiers were killed in an attack on the Khobar military base in Saudi Arabia. The United States accused Osama bin Laden of being its instigator. In response, he turned the *jihad* against the USA and Israel in his famous epistle, entitled *"Expel the Polytheists from the Arabian Peninsula"*. He took up the same type of arguments that he had utilized with the CIA in Afghanistan: it was the sacred duty of all Muslims to liberate Islam's occupied territories. But it is difficult to compare the bloody Soviet occupation of Afghanistan with the contractual installation of U.S.

military bases in Saudi Arabia. The millionaire's exhortation not finding the echo hoped for among the Muslim popular masses, in 1998 he created, with the Egyptian leader Ayman Al-Zawahiri, the Islamic International Front Against Jews and Crusaders.

On 7 August 1998, attacks devastated the American embassies in Dar-es-Salaam (Tanzania) and Nairobi (Kenya), resulting in 299 deaths and over 4,500 injured. The United States accused Osama bin Laden of being the instigator. President Bill Clinton ordered 75 cruise missiles to be fired at the Jalalabad and Khost training camps in Afghanistan, as well as the Al-Shifa laboratory in Sudan. The FBI brought charges against bin Laden and set a price of five million dollars upon his head. All of his financial assets were frozen.

On 12 October 2000 an attack using a dinghy loaded with explosives damaged the destroyer *USS Cole* anchored off Aden (Yemen), killing seventeen sailors and wounding thirty-nine others. The United States accused Osama bin Laden of being the sponsor.

On 8 May 2001, Donald Rumsfeld revealed that the Public Enemy N° 1 of the United States not only already possessed bacteriological and chemical weapons, but he was also on the verge of assembling an atomic bomb and launching a satellite.

Interviewed by the PBS program, *Frontline*[109], Milton Bearden (former CIA bureau chief in Sudan during the 1980's and of the principal figures in the Agency's secret operations in Afghanistan) expressed his skepticism: *"To oversimplify it by linking him* [Osama bin Laden] *to every known terrorist act in the last decade is an insult* [to the intelligence] *of most Americans. And it certainly doesn't encourage our allies in this to take us very seriously."* Milton Bearden, who regained his freedom to speak on such matters following his retirement in 1994, went on to say: *"There's a lot of fiction in there. But we like that. It's the whole Osama bin Laden mythology. It's almost part entertainment. We haven't had a national enemy since the evil empire* [the USSR] *slipped beneath the waves in 1991. And I think we kind of like this way. We like this whole international terrorist thing oddly enough at a time when it* [real terrorism] *is changing its character dramatically."*

In any case, *"the show must go on"*: the USA accused Osama bin Laden of being behind the attacks on 11 September 2001. Invited on *Meet the Press* (NBC), and in the face of skepticism being voiced by foreign ministries in other countries, the Secretary of State, General Colin Powell, declared: : *"We are hard at work bringing all the information together, intelligence information, law enforcement information. And I think, in the near future, we will be able to put out a paper, a document, that will describe quite clearly the evidence that we have linking him to this attack."*[110] Announced several times, this document has never been published.

On October 4, the British Prime Minister, Tony Blair, presented to the House of Commons a report entitled *Responsibility for the Terrorist Atrocities in the United States.*[111]

The sole real argument one finds therein is that *"no other organization has both the motivations and the capacity to conduct attacks like those of September 11, except the Al-Qaeda network led by Osama bin Laden."*

The same day, the Pakistani Foreign Minister, Riaz Muhammad Khan, declared the American *"evidence"* transmitted to his government *"furnished sufficient basis to bring* [bin Laden] *to trial*". This *"evidence"*, classified top secret, has never been made public.

On October 7, the American and British ambassadors informed the UN of the military action their two countries had commenced in Afghanistan.[112] John Negroponte wrote: *"My government has obtained clear and irrefutable information that the Al-Qaeda organization, that is supported by the Taliban regime in Afghanistan, has played a central role in the attacks."* This *"clear and irrefutable"* information has never been transmitted to the Security Council.

On November 10, the *Sunday Telegraph* revealed the existence of a video cassette (recorded on October 20) on which Osama bin Laden claimed responsibility for the attacks: *"The Twin Towers were legitimate targets. They constituted pillars of American economic power. These events were grandiose from all points of review. It was not only the Twin Towers, but the towers of that country's morale which were destroyed."* Bin Laden was also said to have threatened the American President and the British Prime Minister. *"Bush and Blair do not understand anything but relative power. Each time they kill us, we kill them, so that a balance of forces is reached."* These revelations were confirmed the same day by Tony Blair, who indicated to the House of Commons that he had seen a transcript of the tape. This mysterious cassette was cited in the updated version of Blair's report.[113] It was in an interview given to the al-Jazeera news network, and later broadcast by CNN in January 2002.

In a dramatic turn of events, on December 9 the *Washington Post* announced on its front page the existence of a new video cassette.[114] Recorded by a close associate of the Public Enemy N° 1 on September 11, it showed the reactions of Osama bin Laden and definitively certified his responsibility in the planning of the attacks. According to *Reuters*, citing an anonymous source, the leader of Al-Qaeda even indicated on the tape that most of the hijackers weren't kamikazes and were unaware that they would be sacrificed.

Invited on the program *This Week* (ABC), the Deputy Defense Secretary, Paul Wolfowitz, commented: *"It's repugnant. I mean here is a man who takes pride and pleasure from killing thousands of innocent human beings. This confirms what we already know about him. There's nothing new or surprising in there. It's only a confirmation. And I hope it will finally put a stop to these insane conspiracy theories according to which in some way the United States or somebody else are the guilty parties."*[115]

The cassette was released by the Pentagon on 13 December 2001. Osama bin Laden delivers "confessions" on the tape that correspond on every point with the official version that we know is far from the truth. *"I was thinking that the fire from the gas in the plan would melt the iron structure of the* [WTC] *building and collapse the area where the plane had hit and all the floors above it only. This is all we had hoped for* [...] *We had finished our work that day and the radio on* [...] *We turned the radio station to the news from Washington. The news continued and no mention of the attack until the end. At the end of the newscast, they reported that a plane just hit the World Trade Center* [...] *After a little while, they announced that another plane had hit the World Trade Center. The brothers who heard the news were overjoyed by it.* [...] *The brothers, who conducted*

the operation, all they knew was that they have a mar-
tyrdom operation and we asked each of them to go to
America but they didn't know anything about the opera-
tion, not even one letter. But they were trained and we
did not reveal the operation to them until they are there
and just before they boarded the planes [...] They were
overjoyed when the first plane hit the building, so I said
to them: be patient [...] The difference between the first
and the second plane hitting the towers was twenty
minutes. And the difference between the first plane and
the plane that hit the Pentagon was one hour."[116]

Not only does the agent bin Laden credit the fables of the towers' collapse due to the effects of combustion, that of the kamikaze teams, and even that of the Pentagon plane crash, but he also takes care to deny the obvious. Indeed, the video closes with this commentary by his acolyte: *"They* [the Americans] *were terrified, thinking there was a coup"*. If the Public Enemy N° 1 of the United States says so...

*   *   *

The guilt of the repeat offender Osama bin Laden in the attacks of September 11 is thus beyond question because he has confessed to actions that never happened. But did bin Laden really break with the CIA and become an enemy of America?

From 1987 to 1998, the training of Al-Qaeda's fighters was supervised by Ali Mohammed, an Egyptian officer incorporated into the United States military. At the same time, Mohammed also taught at the John F. Kennedy Special Warfare Center and School, where he trained members of the most secret network of US influence, the *"stay-behind"*, as well as officers of the US Special Forces.[117] In light of the security regulations of the American secret services, which call for constant surveillance of its agents, can one believe for a single instant that Ali Mohammed could alternate between a military base in the USA and Al-Qaeda camps in Sudan and Afghanistan without being immediately unmasked? The widely publicized arrest of Ali Mohammed at the end of 1998 does not suffice to hide the fact that this *"stay-behind"* agent trained Al-Qaeda's fighters and that therefore Osama bin Laden continued to work for the CIA at least until 1998!

How can one not see that Osama bin Laden legend is a cover story fabricated out of whole cloth by the CIA? They even tried to convince us that bin Laden kicked the most powerful army in the world out of Somalia with only twenty fighters!

Or to give another example, the attacks in Nairobi and Dar-es-Salaam were presented as anti-American, but none of the eleven dead in Dar-es-Salaam were from the United States, while in Nairobi only twelve of the 213 dead were American. Those who staged these falsely anti-American attacks took care to ensure that the consequences were borne by others.[118]

In reality, the CIA continued to have recourse to Osama bin Laden's services against Russian influence as it had done against the Soviets. You don't change a winning team. The "Arab Legion" of Al-Qaeda was used, in 1999, to support the Kosovar rebels against the dictatorship in Belgrade.[119] It was also operational in Chechenya, at least until November 2001, as was attested to by the *New York Times*.[120] The alleged hostility of bin Laden against the United States permitted Washington to deny responsibility for these "dirty operations". The links bet-ween the CIA and bin Laden were not severed in 1998. Seriously ill, he went for treatment from 4 to 14 July 2001 at the American Hospital in Dubai (United Arab Emirates). *"During his hospitalization [he] received visits from several members of his family and other important persons from Saudi Arabia and the Emirates. During this same stay, the local representative of the CIA, who is a well-known figure in Dubai, was seen taking the main elevator to visit Osama's room"* the French newspaper *Le Figaro* revealed.[121] And a CBS correspondent reported that *"the night before the Sept. 11 terrorists attack, Osama bin Laden was in Pakistan. He was getting medical treatment with the support of the very military that days later pledged its backing for the U.S. war on terror in Afghanistan [...] Bin Laden was spirited into a military hospital in Rawalpindi for kidney dialysis treatment."*[122]

The man who launched a *jihad* against the USA and Israel, the man on whose head the FBI offered a bounty of five million dollars, the man whose training camps were bombarded by cruise missiles, was treated in an American hospital in Dubai, where he chatted with the local CIA bureau chief, then underwent dialysis while under the protection of the Pakistani army in Rawalpindi.

The hoax implicates both close associates of bin Laden and Al-Qaeda fighters. For example, according to the official American version, the Al-Shifa laboratory in Sudan was supposedly used by bin Laden to manufactu-re chemical weapons of mass destruction. For that rea-son, it was bombarded by the U.S. Air Force in 1998. Nevertheless, international observers who arrived to inspect the ruins found that it produced nothing other than aspirin. The factory belonged jointly to Osama bin Laden and to Salah Idris. The CIA accused the latter of complicity in the fabrication of chemical weapons and the funding of Islamic Jihad in Egypt. It had his financial assets frozen, but then lifted the measure discreetly in May 1999. The *"terrorist"* Salah Idris today controls 75% of IES Digital Systems and 20% of Protec through the intermediary of the offshore company Global Security Systems. Now, IES Digital Systems provides video surveillance for a number of British governmental and military sites, as Baroness Cox revealed to the House of Commons, while Protec assures security for eleven British nuclear power plants.[123]

As for Mohammed Atta, who the FBI accuses of being the Al-Qaeda agent who led the kamikaze commandos on September 11 and whose bank account was used to finance the operation, he was an agent of Pakistan's Inter-Service Intelligence (ISI) – who have always been considered as a branch of the CIA.[124] In July 2001, General Ahmed Mahmud, the ISI director, transferred one hundred thousand dollars to Mohammed Atta's bank account in the United States, the *Times of India* reported.[125] This revelation raised no questions in the USA. At most, General Mahmud was asked to take his retirement, but only after having designated his own successor.

The measures adopted by the USA against bin Laden were not convincing, either. The seventy-five cruise missiles[126] fired against Al-Qaeda's training camps and the Al-Shifa factory killed only twenty-one Islamic fighters, which does not seem proportionate, either to the means utilized, or to the 298 dead in Nairobi and Dar-es-Salaam.

*"Since the Cold War era, Washington has delibe-
rately supported Osama bin Laden, while placing him on
the FBI's most wanted list. While* mujahiddin *are implicated in armed insurrections on behalf of the United
States in the Balkans and the former USSR, the FBI has
the mission to bring him to the US and to carry out a war
on terrorism. By all appearances, it's not only a matter
of contradictory actions, but a policy of lying to citizens,
because since the USSR-Afghanistan war the CIA has
supported international terrorism through its secret operations"* [127] writes Professor Michel Chossudovsky of
the University of Ottawa.

* * *

On the one hand, bin Laden is not an enemy but
an agent of the United States; on the other, he never
broke with his family, who are an essential commercial
partner of the Bush family.[128]

We have already indicated that the financial assets
of the Saudi Binladen Group (SBG) are managed by the
Carlyle Group.

Created in 1987, the Carlyle Group today over-
sees a portfolio worth twelve billion dollars. It holds a
majority of shares in Seven Up (who are the bottlers for
Cadbury Schweppes), Federal Data Corporation (who,
for example, equipped the Federal Aviation Authority
with its surveillance system for civilian air traffic), and
United Defense Industries Inc. (major suppliers of the
American, Turkish, and Saudi Arabian armies). Through
the companies that it controls, the Carlyle Group is ranked
11th biggest among American armaments companies.

In 1990, the Carlyle Group was implicated in an affair involving the extortion of funds. A lobbyist for the Republican Party, Wayne Berman, had obtained money from American retirement funds to finance the election campaigns of the Bush family; one of these funds had agreed to pay one million dollars to the Carlyle Group in exchange for a public contract in Connecticut.

The Group is presided over by Frank C. Carlucci (former deputy director of the CIA, before becoming Secretary of Defense). He is advised by James A. Baker II (former White House Chief of Staff under President Reagan, then Secretary of the Treasury, and finally Secretary of State under George Bush senior). To represent the Group in other countries, the Carlyle Group employs John Major[129] (former British Prime Minister) and George Bush senior[130] (former CIA director, then President of the United States).

Among the other directors of the Carlyle Group, one finds Sami Mubarak Baarma, the agent of Khaled bin Mafouz, and a certain Talat Othman. Both figures are directly linked to the current President of the United States.

Indeed, George W. Bush derives his own personal fortune from the profitable business he did at the head of Harken Energy Corporation.[131] This small Texan oil company won petroleum concessions from Bahrein, as a kickback for contracts with Kowait negotiated by George Bush senior.[132] A totally illegal operation, to be sure.

Khaled bin Mafouz was a shareholder in Harken to the tune of 11.5%. His shares were "handled" by one of his proxies, Abdullah Taha Baksh. Talat Othman was administrator, while the elder brother of Osama bin Laden, Salem, was represented on Harken's board of directors by his American agent, James R. Bath.

The members of this tight little circle (the Bush family, their political cronies and financial partners, plus the inevitable CIA) are not novices in the matter of manipulations. They were at the center of the biggest financial scandal of the 1990's: the BCCI bankruptcy.[133]

The Bank of Credit and Commerce International (BCCI) was an Anglo-Pakistani establishment present in seventy-three countries. It was jointly owned by three great families: the Gokal (Pakistan), the bin Mafouz (Saudi Arabia) and the Geith Pharaon[134] (Abu Dhabi).

It was also used by Ronald Reagan to corrupt the Iranian government so that it delayed the liberation of the American hostages in Teheran embassy and so sabotaged the end of Jimmy Carter's presidency (the so-called "October Surprise"). Then, at the urging of former CIA director and Vice President Bush (senior), the Reagan administration again used the BCCI to transfer Saudi donations to the *Contras* in Nicaragua, and also to channel CIA funds to the *mujahiddin* in Afghanistan. The BCCI was implicated as well in the arms deals of Syrian dealer Sarkis Sarkenalian, the Keatinga scandal in the U.S., in the affairs of financier Marc Rich, in the funding of the Abu Nidal group, etc. Finally, the bank failed when it was established that it also laundered the money of the Medellin Cartel. A million small depositors lost their savings when it closed its doors.

The fact that the BCCI could be manipulated, if not created, by the CIA, shouldn't come as a surprise. There is a long banking tradition within the American secret services ever since the foundation of the OSS by Wall Street business lawyers and stockbrokers. Two former CIA directors, Richard Helms and William Casey, worked for the BCCI, as did two influential agents:

Adnan Khasshoggi[135] (representative of the Saudi Binladen Group in the USA) and Manucher Ghobanifar (the principal trader in the Irangate affair). Not to mention Kamal Adham (brother-in- law of King Faisal and head of the Saudi secret services until 1977), Prince Turki Al-Faisal Al-Saud (chief of the Saudi secret services from 1977 to August 2001, and tutor of Osama bin Laden) and Abdul Raouf Khalil (deputy director of the Saudi secret services).

Just to keep the record straight, one should note that the BCCI also seems to have played a secret role in France. It notably served to disguise the transfer of Franco-American technology to Pakistan and to pay for the liberation of hostages. Dominique Santini, a businessman close to Charles Pasqua who was indicted abroad for his role within the BCCI[136], independently of charges against him in France in the Elf-Thinet affair. Three years after the bank's collapse, its former directors were involved as intermediaries in the negotiation of the Sawari-II contract and organized a system of kickbacks which supposedly financed French Prime Minister Edouard Balladur's election campaign. The questions raised by this sale of gunboats to Saudi Arabia led Jacques Chirac, upon his assuming office as President in the Elysees Palace, to order the wire-tapping of former French Defense Minister François Léotard.

The BCCI operated in close collaboration with SICO[137], the Swiss investment subsidiary of the Saudi Binladen Group, which included among its administrators, Salem, one of the brothers of Osama bin Laden.

Held partially responsible for the bankruptcy of BCCI, Khalid bin Mahfouz was indicted in the United States in 1992. He managed to have the charges against him dropped in 1995, however, after a transaction with the bank's creditors entailing payment of 245 million dollars.

* * *

If it is true, as many American officials claim, that the bin Laden family continues to maintain relations with Osama and to finance his political activities, then the Carlyle Group, which manages the financial investments of the Saudi Binladen Group, would necessarily be implicated in the insider trading mentioned previously. George Bush senior would thus be one of the happy beneficiaries of the stock exchange maneuvers of 11 September 2001. That alone would be a good reason for the FBI and the IOSCO to close down the financial aspects of the investigation.

Chapter 9

BUSINESS AS USUAL

On 7 October 2001, George W. Bush delivered a solemn address on television. His speech was not broadcast from the Oval Office, but from the Treaty Room of the White House: the war had started.[138]

"On my orders, the United States military has begun strikes against Al-Qaeda terrorist training camps and military installations of the Taliban regime in Afghanistan. These carefully targeted actions are designed to disrupt the use of Afghanistan as a terrorist base of operations, and to attack the military capability of the Taliban regime.

We are joined in this operation by our staunch friend, Great Britain. Other close friends, including Canada, Australia, Germany and France, have pledged forces as the operation unfolds. More than 40 countries in the Middle East, Africa, Europe and across Asia have granted air transit or landing rights. Many more have shared intelligence. We are supported by the collective will of the world.

More than two weeks ago, I gave Taliban leaders a series of clear and specific demands: Close terrorist trai-

ning camps; hand over leaders of the Al-Qaeda network; and return all foreign nationals, including American citizens, unjustly detained in your country. None of these demands were met. And now the Taliban will pay a price.

[...] the oppressed people of Afghanistan will know the generosity of America and our allies. As we strike military targets, we'll also drop food, medicine and supplies to the starving and suffering men and women and children of Afghanistan.

The United States of America is a friend to the Afghan people, and we are the friends of almost a billion worldwide who practice the Islamic faith. The United States of America is an enemy of those who aid terrorists and of the barbaric criminals who profane a great religion by committing murder in its name.

[...]We did not ask for this mission, but we will fulfill it."

In London, Tony Blair addressed the British people from 10 Downing Street. He confirmed that Her Majesty's troops fought side-by-side with the Americans.

As fire rained down upon Kabul, the Qatari non-stop news network Al-Jazeera broadcast a pre-recorded response from Osama bin Laden[139]: "*Here is America struck by Allah in its most vulnerable point, destroying, thank Allah, its most prestigious buildings and we thank Allah for that. Here is America filled with terror from north to south and from east to west, and we thank Allah for that. Allah has guided the footsteps of a group of Muslims, a vanguard that has destroyed America and we implore Allah to elevate their rank and receive them in Paradise.*

[...] After what has happened and after what the leaders of the United States, in the front ranks of whom is Bush, the chief of the world's unbelievers, have said and after they mobilized their men and their horses (sic) *and dressed against us countries that pretend to be Muslim [...] they have come out to do battle with a group which holds to its religion and is disinterested in this world, they have come out to combat Islam and to aggress its peoples with the pretext of terrorism.*

[...] These events have divided the entire world in two parts: those who have the faith and are without hypocrisy and those who are unbelievers may God preserve us from them. Every Muslim must rise up to defend his religion because the wind of the faith and the change has blown to annihilate the injustice in the peninsula of Mahomet [the Arabian peninsula, where the prophet of Islam was born].

To America I address measured words, I swear by Allah that America will never again know security before Palestine knows it and before all the atheist Western armies leave the holy lands [of Islam].

This dialogue via the media between President Bush and the CIA agent Osama bin Laden having confirmed to the world that the war in Afghanistan was in fact a riposte to the September 11 attacks, the real business could begin.

* * *

The collapse of the USSR and the independence of the former Soviet states of Central Asia reopened the "Great Game".[140] The expression, first coined by Rudyard Kipling in the 19th Century, designates the struggles for influence that the great powers have waged in the region, while avoiding direct confrontation as far as possible

The region contains very important reserves of oil and gas. In the mountains, one also finds precious stones. And opium is grown there.[141]

Upon reaching the White House, George W. Bush composed his governmental team with the top people in the oil lobby. Thus, the National Security adviser, Condoleezza Rice[142], is a former director of Chevron-Texaco[143], while the Secretary of the Interior, Gale Norton, represents the interests of BP-Amoco[144] and those of the Saudi company Delta Oil. From 29 January 2001, Vice President Cheney – formerly president of Halliburton[145] (the largest oil equipment supplier in the world) – set up the National Energy Policy Development (NEPD) group. Its meetings take place under tight security, the list of participants is a state secret, and the taking of written minutes is forbidden. Everything surrounding it is so mysterious that the *Washington Post* soon said that it was "*a sort of secret society*".[146]

Commentators – who were unaware at that point of the coming bankruptcy of Enron, the world's largest energy trader – agreed in thinking that the primordial objective of the NEPD was to exploit the hydrocarbon reserves of the Caspian Sea. The question is how to transport the oil and gas without having to negotiate with Russia and Iran. A pipeline will be built to join the Caspian with the Mediterranean by crossing Azerbaijan, Georgia and Turkey (the "BTC" project, for Baku-Tbilissi-Ceyhan). In the meantime, another pipeline has been constructed linking the Caspian to the Black Sea, but unhappily this passes through Russia which takes its cut of revenues. It links Tengiz to Novorossisysk and was inaugurated on 27 November 2001. A third, more promising, route would link the Caspian to the Indian Ocean (a project led by the UNOCAL firm with the help of Delta Oil).[147] But there was a big problem with this. The pipeline would not only have to cross Pakistan, but also Afghanistan which had fallen prey to internecine strife after any form of organized state had disappeared with the Soviet debacle. In December 1997, UNOCAL had to suspend its project in view of the incomprehension on the part of the Taliban. All attempts since at unblocking the situation failed, although the company's vice president, John J. Maresca was named U.S. ambassador to Afghanistan.

To re-launch discussions, Secretary of State Colin Powell approved forty-three million dollars in aid to the Taliban regime for the re-conversion of peasant opium growers. After having obtained the accord of the G-8 summit at Genoa (where India participated as an observer), multipartite negotiations were organized in Berlin, bringing together the Americans, British, Pakistanis, Afghans, and Russians. Germany hosted the meeting as it presided the UN contact group on Afghanistan. But with which Afghans would discussions take place? With the legal government of President Rabbani, internationally recognized but no longer controlling most of the country, or with the Islamic Emirate governed by a medieval sect: the Taliban? The decision was taken to invite the latter, in violation of a U.N. Security Council resolution which forbade receiving them. Given valid visas, the Taliban dignitaries made use of their trip to Germany to preach and collect funds in Hamburg.

The Taliban[148] are a closed fraternity; a Sunnite sect that professes the return to a primitive form of Islam. Their leaders are veterans of the war against the Soviets, all of them handicapped during the conflict. They recognize the authority of a rural mullah, Omar, who has never traveled abroad, and does not even know a third of his own country. In the chaos that followed the Soviet withdrawal, the Taliban seized the advantage by making use of ethnic ties: like most of heads of the Pakistani secret services (ISI), they are Pushtuns.

Mullah Omar styled himself Commander of the Faithful and created an Emirate, recognized only by Pakistan, Saudi Arabia, and the United Arab Emirates. Having no training in international relations, they turned to some of their American friends who had provided them aid in fighting against the Soviets. Thus they were represented unofficially at the United Nations by Leila Helms, the niece of Richard Helms (CIA director from 1966 to 1973). In internal politics, the Taliban imposed an iron discipline upon the population, discriminating against women and forbidding impious acts. After having tolerated the cultivation of opium for some while, they then prohibited it, depriving part of the peasantry of any resource. The sect conceded a large portion of territory to Osama bin Laden.

The Taliban, inexperienced in diplomatic niceties, tried to negotiate international recognition of their regime in return for passage of the pipeline. Seeing that this was impossible since the U.N. recognized another government – that of the unsubstantial President Rabbani – they broke off talks. According to the Pakistani diplomat, Niaz Naik, the American delegation became threatening and announced in mid-July that the dispute would be decided by arms.

The United States planned to eliminate the principal leaders of the Afghan factions, whether they be Mullah Omar or Commandant Massoud (whose anti-American sentiments were proverbial) and replace them with a puppet government. It would derive a certain degree of legitimacy from the blessing of the former king, Zaher Shah, a forgotten old monarch spending the last years of his life in exile in Rome.

In mid-July, the great powers gave their approval to this plan. Thus the final communiqué of the meeting on 17 July between Hubert Védrine (the French Foreign Minister) and Francesc Vendrell (head of the U.N. Special Mission for Afghanistan) reads: *"The two officials together explored ways to permit in the end a favorable evolution, in particular the encouragement that the international community might provide to the efforts of the king* (sic) *to gather around him the representatives of Afghan society. They also raised the question of the utility of strengthening dialogue with Pakistan. Beyond, it will naturally also be necessary to reflect on what will be required for the reconstruction of Afghanistan, once the conflict is ended* (sic)."[149]

Yes, from the month of July, they were speaking of the deposed sovereign Zaher Shah as if he were the actual king of Afghanistan, and at the same time were contemplating parallel debates on the *"conflict"* and the *"reconstruction"* of the country!

Negotiations continued, in London then in Geneva, under the cover of the Business Humanitarian Forum[150] (sic) – whose budget is amply fed by the UNOCAL oil company –, but with different objectives and guests (including the Japanese, who expect a great deal from the Caspian oilfields). As Messieurs Védrine and

Vendrell foretold, no one was preparing any longer for peace, but for war and reconstruction.

Fearing overly strong Anglo-American pressure, Pakistan looked for new allies before the storm broke. It invited a Chinese delegation to Islamabad and promised that it would open a doorway for China to the Indian Ocean in exchange for military aid. Irritated, the Anglo-Americans decided to pass even more quickly onto the offensive, in any case before the Chinese could disrupt the Great Game.[151] The Sea of Oman became the theatre of the biggest deployment of the British fleet since the Falklands War, while NATO transported forty thousand troops to Egypt. On September 9, the charismatic leader of the Islamic Front, the very anti-American Commandant Massoud, was assassinated.[152] The attacks of September 11 allowed what was nothing more than a classic colonial expedition to be disguised as a legitimate operation.

* * *

The operation was supposed to be called "*Infinite Justice*", but the effect on public opinion in the Muslim world was deplorable. It thus finally came to be called "*Enduring Freedom*".[153] It was supported by an *ad hoc* diplomatic alliance, a Global Coalition which assembled 134 states[154] that had offered some form of military assistance to the USA.[155] The Americans, recalling how the Soviets became bogged down in a ground conflict during the first Afghan war (1979-1989), abstained from sending in the GI's They preferred to buy the local warlords at a hefty price and use them to fight against the Taliban. This method obviously entailed arming rival factions in violation of the embargo decreed by the UN.

Faced with the new turn of events, the Russians massively supplied weaponry to the Islamic Front of the late Massoud, while Iran aided the Shi'ite Hazaris. The US Air Force contented itself with pinpoint bombings to support the anti-Taliban forces, and sometimes also to contain them. In fact, the war objectives of the fighters from the various factions had no relationship with those proclaimed by the Global Coalition (the arrest of Osama bin Laden), or with the ambitions of the oil companies standing in the wings.

The Anglo-Americans then changed tactics, returning to traditional carpet bombing pulverizing those importunate enough to be below. The Taliban were incapable of maintaining their dictatorship over their territory and found themselves isolated in scattered groups. At the same time, the Islamic Front, re-baptized as the *"Northern Alliance"* for the sake of international communication, broke through the Taliban's disorganized frontlines

The US Air Force then set upon the fleeing enemy troops. The Taliban tried to regroup in Kandahar, while the victors committed several massacres, notably at Mazar-i-Sharif under the command of General Dostum. In the end, one-to-two thousand fanatics, a mixture of Taliban and members of Al-Qaeda, dug into the mountains of Tora-Bora under a deluge of steel, then negotiated their surrender into the hands of their Pakistani friends. In total, the Anglo-American planes carried out 4,700 sorties during which they dropped twelve thousand bombs, killing over ten thousand combatants[156] and *"collaterally"* at least a thousand more civilians.[157] The military escalation led the U.S. Air Force to abandon the theory of *"surgical strikes"* and to use weapons of mass destruction, BLU-82 bombs[158] (the so-called *"daisy cut-*

ters") to neutralize the last fighters scattered in the mountains.

The war ended with Resolution 1378[159] of the U.N. Security Council. It set the framework for the talks in Bonn[160] (Germany) where the various Afghan factions agreed on a new government.[161] The round table put into place a provisional administration that it wanted to be presided over by the former king, Zaher Shah. The latter having declined as was foreseen, it was Hamid Karzai who became Prime Minister. During the war against the Soviets, he was personally linked to the CIA director at that time, William Casey. Afterwards, he emigrated to the United States and became a friend of the Bush family and was employed by a subsidiary of UNOCAL.[162] General Abdel Rachid Dostum, nicknamed *"Genghis Khan"* due to the atrocities of which he has been guilty over the last twenty years, managed to rally the Global Coalition in time. He's done well out of it: not only is he not being prosecuted for war crimes, but he's been integrated into the new administration. The arrangement was validated on 6 December 2001, by Resolution 1383[163] of the Security Council. The hundreds of thousands of Afghans who fled their country to escape the bombings are returning home.

Operation *"Enduring Freedom"* was largely piloted from within the US National Security Council by Zalmay Khalilzad.[164] The son of an advisor to the former king, Zaher Shah, he studied in America at the University of Chicago. He fought inside his country in liaison with the CIA during the war against the USSR before becoming naturalized as a U.S. citizen, with a job as advisor to the State Department under Ronald Reagan. During the presidency of Bush senior, he was appointed

Under-Secretary at Defense and played a key role in Operation *"Desert Storm"* against Iraq. In the Clinton years, he worked for the Rand Corporation and UNO-CAL. When negotiations were progressing with the Taliban, he defended them in the *Washington Post*, writing that they *"never practiced at all that anti-Americanism professed by the Iranian fundamentalists"*. He changed his point of view once the oil pipeline negotiations broke down and he became the primary expert for Afghan matters within the Bush Administration.[165] At the end of the war, he was named special envoy to Afghanistan. In future, he should be overseeing the construction of the much-coveted pipeline.

The international press was invited to visit the vestiges of the installations used by the Taliban and Al-Qaeda. It discovered miserable hovels with piles of weapons inherited from the war against the Soviets. But no journalist stumbled across any factories producing chemical and bacteriological weapons, or the centers for assembling atomic bombs, and still less the bases for launching satellites that Donald Rumsfeld had warned about.

The greatest army in the world, for its part, was unable to find the alleged Public Enemy N° 1 it was sent to arrest, while Mullah Omar escaped to Pakistan on a motorbike.

It's back to business as usual. The opium crop destined for the North American market can finally spread freely.[166] And on 9 February 2002, Hamid Karzai and his Pakistani counterpart, General Musharraf, at long last concluded an accord for the construction of the Central Asian pipeline.[167]

Chapter 10

SECRET OPERATIONS

In a note written by Leonard Wong for the Institute of Strategic Studies of the US Army entitled '*Maintaining Public Support for Military Operations*'[168], one reads: "*Public support for military action is at levels that parallel the public reaction after the attack at Pearl Harbor. Americans claim today that they believe military action is appropriate, that they support a protracted war, and that they are willing to endure the negative consequences that may accompany the war. Despite the favorable polls, Americans are bound to be fickle in their support [...] Americans are being told to return to their normal lives – lives that largely ignored the military before the attacks. As they return to those lives, their support of military action will diminish unless the military continually shows progress in the war against terrorism, keeps the nation connected to its armed forces, and provides domestic security that is effective, but for the most part unseen.*" In other words, public opinion will adhere massively to the American war policy as long as the suspense lasts.

Operation "*Enduring Freedom*" commenced on 7 October 2001. The sound of cannons moved off into Central Asia. Given the relative strengths of the opposing sides, the victory of the Coalition was assured before battle was even joined. The attention of the American public began to waver. Indeed, Al-Qaeda's hideaways were under attack and Osama bin Laden had threatened America on television, but no new terrorist actions by the *"sleeper networks"* implanted on American territory had been reported. People began to doubt the reality of the menace. So, what do you think happened?

On October 12, the press agencies circulated some alarming information. Journalists and members of Congress had received letters poisoned with anthrax. All in all, five booby-trapped letters were sent to the *National Enquirer*, to NBC, to the *New York Post*, and to the offices of Senators Daschle and Leahy. They resulted in five deaths. The normal, everyday life of Americans came to a halt. They could no longer open their mail without gloves and a handkerchief over their noses. The suppliers of gas masks and survival kits ran out of stocks. The entire postal system was paralyzed. The psychosis spread to allied countries. Throughout Europe, letters were discovered containing the fatal white powder: Al-Qaeda had decided to go on the offensive and to use chemical and biological weapons it had amassed thanks to technical aid from Saddam Hussein. The United States and its allies built up stocks of vaccine against anthrax. They stimulated the pharmaceutical industry from whom they ordered millions of doses. And then nothing. Except for the five letters, it all turned out to be pranks and collective hallucination.

The fact remains that the five letters contained a militarized form of anthrax that had been produced in the laboratories of the United States. The menace was internal. Barbara Hatch Rosenberg of the Federation of American Scientists noted that only fifty researchers – all of them readily identifiable – had access to such strains and were in a position to manipulate them.[169] An anonymous letter, addressed to the Quantico military base at the end of September – i.e. before the press was informed of the anthrax attacks - denounced the activities of a former researcher with US AMRIID, Dr. Asaad. The FBI once again wrung its hands and failed to elucidate matters.

Now that the panic has passed and the lightning operation of *"Enduring Freedom"* is over, the public believes that it can turn the page. But the Defense Department has taken on the task of keeping the menace fresh in people's minds. Providing powerful TV footage, *"particularly dangerous terrorists"* have been imprisoned in the military base of Guantanamo (Cuba). They were brought by plane from Afghanistan after having been drugged and chained to their seats. Once delivered, they were subjected to a program of sensory deprivation: eyes blindfolded, ears muffled, noses plugged. The legal experts at the Defense Department[170] explained without turning a hair that only federal laws forbade the practice of torture, and these did not apply to Guantanamo[171], situated outside US territory. As for the Constitution, it says nothing on the subject. The French general, Paul Aussaresses, who admitted having organized torture in Algeria and later offered up his morbid expertise to the American special forces, learnedly explained the uses of torture on television.[172] The *"International Community"* was roused. Mary Robinson, the UN High Commissioner for Human Rights (and former President of the Republic of Eire) became publicly indignant and called the American government to task:[173] the detainees have the status of prisoners-of-war as defined by the Geneva

Conventions. They should be treated humanely, and their trials must be fair and equitable.

* * *

While public opinion trembled and grew passionate, the *"war on terrorism"* began in the shadows. But terrorism is neither a state, nor an organization, nor a doctrine; it's a mode of action. It can be employed just as well by governments (Robespierre's dictatorship in France during 1793 was called *"the Terror"*) as it can by minorities in opposition. Terrorism is sometimes fully justified. Thus, during the Second World War, the French Resistance engaged in terrorist actions against the forces of occupation and collaboration, both civilian and military. The expression *"war on terrorism"* has no more meaning than *"war on war"*.

It is true that George W. Bush has a highly limited conception of terrorism. Thus, he does not consider the action of death squads in Nicaragua to be *"terrorism"*, to the extent of appointing the *Contras'* former protector, John Negroponte, United States ambassador to the UN.[174] For Bush, in a world become mono-polar since the dissolution of the USSR, terrorism seems to be defined as any form of violent opposition to American leadership.

Based on leaks from several participants and after having consulted the minutes, Bob Woodward (one of the reporters who broke the Watergate scandal) described in great detail in the *Washington Post* the meeting of the Bush Cabinet during which the CIA obtained unlimited powers to pursue the *"secret war against terrorism"*.[175] It took place on 15 September 2001, during a governmental seminar held at Camp David.

The meeting began; of course, with a moment of prayer led by George W. Bush, during which each person present was invited to participate in turn. Then, the Secretary of the Treasury and the Secretary of State outlined their respective actions. The CIA director, George Tenet, next presented two projects accompanied by particularly well-prepared documentation. The first was entitled *"Initial Hook: Destroying al Qaeda, Closing the Safe Haven"*. Tenet described the need for secret operations against Al-Qaeda, not only in Afghanistan, but throughout the world, if necessary in cooperation with the services of undemocratic countries. Having obtained the assent of all those presents, he demanded certain powers indispensable for achieving that goal. *"Tenet wanted a broad, general intelligence order that would allow the CIA to conduct the necessary covert operations without having to come back for formal approval for each specific operation. Tenet said he needed the new authority to allow the agency to operate without restraint – and he wanted encouragement from the president to take risks. Tenet had with him a draft of a presidential intelligence order that would give the CIA power to use the full range of covert instruments, including deadly force [...] Another proposal was that the CIA increase liaison work with key foreign intelligence services. Tenet hoped to obtain the assistance of these agencies with some of the hundreds of millions of dollars in new funding he was seeking. Using such intelligence services as surrogates could triple or quadruple the CIA's effectiveness. Like much of the world of covert activity, these kinds of arrangements carried risks. It would put the United States in league with questionable agencies, some with dreadful human rights records. Some of these intelligence services had a reputation for ruthlessness and they used torture to obtain confessions."*

The meeting continued on a more relaxed note, with Tenet outlining his strategy in Afghanistan. Then, recovering his breath, he presented the second document. It was entitled *"Worldwide Attack Matrix"*, *"which described covert operations in 80 countries that were either underway or that he was now recommending. The actions ranged from routine propaganda to lethal covert action in preparation for military attacks."* Rumsfeld, surmounting the traditional rivalry between the CIA and the Pentagon, warmly approved this. *"When the CIA director finished his presentation, Bush left no doubt what he thought of it, virtually shouting with enthusiasm:* 'Great job'.*"*

This secret war has already begun. In the shadows, the CIA has struck here and there throughout the world at the opponents to George W. Bush's policies. The reporter Wayne G. Madsen has identified four famous victims:[176]

– On 11 November 2001, the leader of West Irian (the portion of the island of New Guinea controlled by Indonesia), Theys Eluay, was kidnapped by a special unit of the Indonesian army, the KOPASSUS. This unit, implicated in the massacres of East Timor, was trained by the American *"stay-behind"* and is supervised by the CIA. Theys Eluay militated for the independence of his country and was opposed to the pillage of its mining resources by Freeport McMoran, a Louisiana-based company of which Dr. Kissinger himself is a director emeritus.

– On 23 December 2001, Chef Bola Ige, the Nigerian Minister of Justice, was assassinated in his bedroom by unidentified commandos. He had been an unlucky presidential candidate of the pan-Yoruba Alliance for Democracy and opposed the privileges extended to Chevron (of which Condoleezza Rice had been a director) and ExxonMobil.[177]

– In January 2002, the governor of the province of Aceh (Indonesia) addressed a letter to the leader of the Aceh Liberation Movement, Abdullah Syaffi, to propose that he participate in peace negotiations. Syaffi did not only demand independence for his province, but also opposed drilling by ExxonMobil. Preaching nonviolence – he was a member of UNPO in the Netherlands – he had gone underground. The letter contained a bug that permitted the satellites of the National Security Agency to locate him. He was assassinated on January 22 by a KOPASSUS squad.

– The extreme rightwing leader of the Lebanese Christian militias, Elie Hobeika, and his bodyguards died on January 24 in a car bombing. Hobeika, who was the principal figure responsible for the massacre of Sabra and Chatila (1982), had turned against Israel and intended to testify against Ariel Sharon at the trial being brought against the latter in Belgium for crimes against humanity. The operation is said to have been prepared jointly by the CIA and Mossad.[178]

You say it's a *"struggle against terrorism"*?

* * *

The *Washington Post* dated February 13 published a long opinion piece written by Dr. Henry Kissinger.[179] The great inspirer of US foreign policy related the debates going on in the nation's capital. Three options are possible after the victory in Afghanistan.

Firstly, one could consider the job to have been done and that the lesson had been learned by anyone tempted to imitate the Taliban; secondly, one could put pressure on certain states that are complaisant with terrorists, such as Sudan or Yemen; or thirdly, one could concentrate on overthrowing Saddam Hussein in Iraq to demonstrate the continuity of American will and to modify the regional balance of power in the Middle East.

Henry Kissinger went on to advocate a decisive attack on Iraq, combining a deployment of force and support for the Iraqi opposition.

The initial test having proved positive, the Bush administration moved into full gear.

On January 29, the President of the United States delivered the tradition "State of the Union" speech before Congress, on this occasion in the presence of the Prime Minister of the Afghan transitional government. He announced the new objectives of the "war on terrorism":

Our nation will continue to be steadfast and patient and persistent in the pursuit of two great objectives. First, we will shut down terrorist camps, disrupt terrorist plans, and bring terrorists to justice. And, second, we must prevent the terrorists and regimes who seek chemical, biological or nuclear weapons from threatening the United States and the world.

Our military has put the terror training camps of Afghanistan out of business, yet camps still exist in at

*least a dozen countries. A terrorist underworld — inclu-
ding groups like Hamas, Hezbollah, Islamic Jihad,
Jaish-i-Mohammed — operates in remote jungles and
deserts, and hides in the centers of large cities.*

   [...]

*Our second goal is to prevent regimes that spon-
sor terror from threatening America or our friends and
allies with weapons of mass destruction.*

   *Some of these regimes have been pretty quiet
since September the 11th. But we know their true nature.
North Korea is a regime arming with missiles and weapons of mass destruction, while starving its citizens.*

   *Iran aggressively pursues these weapons and
exports terror, while an unelected few repress the Iranian
people's hope for freedom.*

   *Iraq continues to flaunt its hostility toward Ameri-
ca and to support terror. The Iraqi regime has plotted to
develop anthrax, and nerve gas, and nuclear weapons for
over a decade. This is a regime that has already used poi-
son gas to murder thousands of its own citizens — leaving
the bodies of mothers huddled over their dead children.
This is a regime that agreed to international inspections
— then kicked out the inspectors. This is a regime that has
something to hide from the civilized world.*

   *States like these, and their terrorist allies, constitute
an axis of evil, arming to threaten the peace of the world."*

For the allies of the United States, the pressure is too
strong. It had now been five months that they had been forced to tow the American line in silence. No decent criticism
of the United States' drift had been possible during the period of mourning that followed the attacks of September 11.
And the USA have been careful indeed to export this mour-

ning to their allies and prolong it by all sorts of commemorative ceremonies and televised shows.

Nevertheless, on February 6 the French Foreign Minister, Hubert Védrine, finally took the bull by the horns.[180] He did so with the backing of his country's President and Prime Minister. On *France Inter* radio he declared:

"We are allies of the United States, and we are friends of this people. We have been sincerely and profoundly united with them in this tragedy of September 11, in the face of this terrorist attack. We are committed, as are a great many other governments, to the struggle against terrorism. Not only out of solidarity with the American people; there is a logic in this and we have to extirpate this evil. We also have to treat its roots. And we are threatened today by a new simplistic response which reduces all the problems to the sole struggle against terrorism. That is not being serious.

[...]

We can't reduce all the problems of the world to the struggle against terrorism – even if it is indispensable to fight terrorism – with military means alone. We have to treat the roots. We have to deal with situations of poverty, of injustice, of humiliation, etc.

[...]

Europe needs to be herself. If we don't agree with American policies, we should say so. We can say that and we should say that [...] To be a friend of the American people, the ally of the United States within the Atlantic Alliance, does not mean to say we are aligned. It does not mean to say that we have renounced all thoughts of our own on any matters.

[...]

We are going to have a dialogue with the United States, we are going to do so out of friendship. We don't ask that United States stay at home, on the contrary. We want the United States to commit themselves in the world, because there are no serious problems that can be resolved without the United States. We ask that they commit themselves but that they commit themselves on the basis of multilateralism, of partnership, and that we can talk with them. If we have to raise our voices a little so that we are heard, then we will do so."

In Washington, Colin Powell greeted the French minister's remarks with condescension and gibed at *"Parisian intellectuals and their dizzy spells"*.

Two days later, the French Prime Minister, Lionel Jospin, seized the opportunity of a meeting of the heads of the European Union's parliaments to drive the same message home before an international audience[181]:

"Following the attacks of September 11, we manifested an unstinting solidarity with the United States and contributed at their side to the response called for by that aggression. This common action against terrorism will be pursued with determination. But that does not at all mean that we should not reflect in a lucid fashion on the lessons that should be drawn from the events of September 11. One cannot in effect reduce the world's problems to the sole dimension of the fight against terrorism – despite its imperious necessity –, or count only on the predominance of military methods to resolve them.

Our conception of the world aims to construct a more balanced international community, a safer and more just world. This conception is founded on a multilateral approach. It relies on all the forms of cooperation that permit members of the international community to tackle together the underlying problems, because none of them can presume to resolve them alone [...] We wish for the United States, without giving in to the strong temptation of unilateralism, to reengage themselves on this path, because without them, the new equilibriums that we are seeking will be more difficult to achieve. For our part, we will continue working to advance these conceptions".

Skepticism is gaining ground in Europe. The next day, it was the turn of Chris Patten (the European commissioner for the Union's foreign relations) to *"break the silence"*. In an interview that appeared in the *Guardian*, he developed on the French criticisms of America's *"absolutist and simplistic positions"*, seasoning them with bittersweet remarks on the need for the United States to listen to their allies: *"Gulliver can't go it alone, and it's not good that we consider ourselves to be Lilliputians who dare not raise our voices."*[182]

On February 10, the contagion took hold in the conference of European foreign ministers, who met in Cuenca (Spain). All of them were united behind the unexpected tandem of Védrine and Patten.

At the NATO summit in Berlin, the revolt was felt within the Alliance itself. The Canadian Prime Minister, Jean Chrétien, reminded listeners that the UN and NATO resolutions only concerned Afghanistan, and that he would not be sympathetic if the United States committed themselves unilaterally in other conflicts.[183]

Are we approaching the moment of truth?

Chapter 11

THE CONSPIRACY

The elements now at our disposal lead us to believe that the attacks of September 11 were masterminded from inside the American state apparatus. Nevertheless, this conclusion shocks and offends us because we had come to believe in the legend of the "bin Laden plot" and because it pains us to contemplate the idea that Americans could cynically sacrifice almost three thousand of their fellow countrymen. And yet, in the past, the United States chiefs of staff have planned – but never carried out – a campaign of terrorism against their own population. That statement demands a reminder of recent history.

* * *

In 1958, the Cuban insurgents led by Colonels Fidel and Raul Castro, Che Guevara, and Camilo Cienfuegos, overturned the puppet regime of Fulgencio Batista. The new government, which was not yet Communist, put an end to the exploitation of the island that a group of US multinationals (Standard Oil, General Motors, ITT, General Electric, Sheraton, Hilton, United Fruit, East Indian Co) and the Bacardi family had ruthlessly indulged in during the previous six years. In retaliation, these companies convinced President Eisenhower to overthrow Castro and his movement.

On 17 March 1960, President Eisenhower approved a *"Program of Covert Operations Against the Castro Regime"* comparable to George Tenet's *"Matrix"*, although limited solely to Cuba. Its goal was *"the replacement of the Castro regime with one more devoted to the true interests of the Cuban people and more acceptable to the U.S., in such a manner to avoid any appearance of U.S. intervention."*[184]

On 17 April 1961, a brigade of Cuban exiles and mercenaries, more or less discreetly organized by the CIA, attempted to disembark at the Bay of Pigs. The operation turned into a fiasco. President John F. Kennedy, who had just arrived in the White House, refused to send the US Air Force in support of the mercenaries. 1,500 men were taken prisoner by the Cuban authorities. Kennedy disavowed the operation and dismissed the CIA director (Allen Dulles), the deputy director (Charles Cabell) and the director of the *"stay-behind"* network (Richard Bissell). He entrusted an internal investigation to his military advisor, General Maxwell Taylor, but no concrete measures came out of this. Kennedy entertained doubts about the attitude of the Joint Chiefs of Staff that had validated the operation knowing that it was bound to fail.[185]

If President Kennedy cracked down on the CIA because of its methods and failures, he did not call into question Washington's policy of hostility towards those in power in Havana. He set up an *"Expanded Special Group"* to plan and conduct the fight against Castro. This group was composed of his brother, Robert Kennedy (the

Attorney General), his military advisor (General Maxwell Taylor), the National Security adviser (McGeorge Bundy), the Secretary of State (Dean Rusk), assisted by an adviser (Alexis Johnson), the Secretary of Defence (Robert McNamara) with his adviser (Roswell Gilpatric), the new CIA director (John McCone) and the Chairman of the Joint Chiefs of Staff (General Lyman L. Lemnitzer)

This Expanded Special Group conceived of a set of secret actions grouped under the generic heading *"Mongoose"*. To carry them out, operational coordination between the State Department, the Department of Defense, and the CIA was entrusted to General Edward Lansdale (assistant to the Secretary of Defense, in charge of special operations, and consequently director of the NSA), while an *ad hoc* unit; *"Group W"* was created within the CIA, under William Harvey.

* * *

In April 1961, the US Army was undergoing a grave crisis: Major General Edwin A. Walker, who had provoked the racial conflicts in Little Rock before taking command of the infantry stationed in Germany, was dismissed by President Kennedy.[186] He was accused of encouraging extreme rightwing proselytizing in the armed forces. He himself was a member of the John Birch Society and the True Knights of the Klu Klux Klan.

The Senate Foreign Affairs Committee carried out an investigation of the extreme right within the military. The hearings were presided over by Senator Albert Gore (Democrat – Tennessee), father of the future American

Vice President. The senators suspected the Chairman of the Joint Chiefs of Staff, Lyman L. Lemnitzer, of participating in the "*Walker plot*".[187] Gore knew that Lemnitzer was a specialist in secret operations: in 1943 he had personally directed the negotiations aimed at turning Italy against the German Third Reich, and then in 1944, together with Allen Dulles he led secret negotiations with the Nazis in Ascona (Switzerland) preparing their surrender (operation Sunrise).[188] He participated in the creation of the "*stay-behind*" network within NATO countries, turning Nazi agents to fight against the USSR, and helped war criminals seeking safe havens in Latin America. But Gore was unable to establish his responsibility in more contemporary events.

A secret correspondence of General Lemnitzer, recently published, shows that he conspired with the commander of American forces in Europe (General Lauris Norstad) and other very high-ranking officers to sabotage John F. Kennedy's policies.

The military extremists denounced Kennedy's refusal to intervene militarily in Cuba. They considered the civilians in the CIA to blame for the poor planning of the Bay of Pigs landings, and President Kennedy a coward for having withheld support from the US Air Force. To unblock the situation, they envisaged furnishing Kennedy with a political pretext for military intervention. This plan, called Operation "*Northwoods*", gave rise to detailed studies that were put into final form by Brigadier General William H. Craig. It was presented to the Expanded Special Group by General Lemnitzer himself, on 13 March 1962. The meeting took place in the office of Secretary of Defense at the Pentagon, from 2:30 to 5:30 pm. It ended badly: Robert McNamara rejected the plan totally, while

General Lemnitzer became threatening. There followed six months of constant hostility between the Kennedy Administration and the Joint Chiefs of Staff, ending with the posting of Lemnitzer as commander of US forces in Europe. Before his departure, the general gave the order to destroy all traces of the Northwoods project, but Robert McNamara kept a copy of the memo submitted to him[189] (included in the Documents & Appendices section of this book).

* * *

The Northwoods operation aimed at convincing the international community that Fidel Castro was irresponsible to the point that he represented a danger to the peace in the West. In order to achieve this result, it was planned to orchestrate, then impute to Cuba, grave damages suffered by the United States. Here are some of the provocations projected:

– Attacking the American base of Guantanamo. The operation would have been conducted by Cuban mercenaries wearing the uniforms of Fidel Castro's forces. It would have included various forms of sabotage and the explosion of a munitions depot, which would necessarily have caused considerable material and human damages.

– Blowing up an American ship in Cuban territorial waters in a manner that would revive the memory of the destruction of the *Maine* (266 dead) in 1898, which led to the American intervention against Spain.[190] In reality, the ship would have been empty and under remote control. The explosion would have been visible from Havana or Santiago to ensure that there were witnesses. Rescue operations would have been conducted in order to render human losses credible. The list of victims would have been published in the press and fake funerals organized to provoke public indignation. The operation would have been triggered when Cuban ships were operating in the zone so as to blame them for the attack.

– Mobilizing states neighboring Cuba by causing them to believe in an invasion threat. A fake Cuban plane would have bombed the Dominican Republic or another state in the region during the night. The bombs utilized would have been, of course, of Soviet origin.

– Mobilizing international public opinion by destroying a manned space flight. In order to have a greater impact on people's minds, the victim would have been John Glenn, the first American to complete an orbit around the Earth (his Mercury flight).

One form of provocation was singled out for particular study: *"It is possible to create an incident which will demonstrate convincingly that a Cuban aircraft has attacked and shot down a chartered civilian airliner en route from the United States to Jamaica, Guatemala, Panama or Venezuela."* A group of passengers who formed part of the plot, who might be students, for example, would have taken a charter flight operated by one of the companies used as fronts for the CIA. Off the coast of Florida, their plane would have crossed with another, in fact an apparent double, but empty and transformed into a drone. The passengers acting as accomplices would have been returned

144

to a CIA base, while the drone would have appeared to continue their trajectory. The aircraft would have transmitted distress messages indicating that it was attacked by Cuban fighters, until it exploded in flight.[191]

The implementation of these plans necessarily implied the deaths of numerous American citizens, both civilian and military. But it was precisely their human cost that made them effective forms of manipulation.

* * *

For John F. Kennedy, Lemnitzer was a hysterical anti-communist supported by unscrupulous multinationals. The new U.S. President understood the meaning of the warning given by his predecessor, President Eisenhower, a year previously, in his address at the end of his two terms in office: *"In the councils of government, we must guard against the acquisition of unwarranted influence, whether sought or unsought, by the military-industrial complex. The potential for the disastrous rise of misplaced power exists and will persist. We must never let the weight of this combination endanger our liberties or democratic processes. We should take nothing for granted. Only an alert and knowledgeable citizenry can compel the proper meshing of the huge industrial and military machinery of defense with our peaceful methods and goals, so that security and liberty may prosper together."*[192]

In the end, John F. Kennedy resisted Generals Walker, Lemnitzer, and their friends, and refused to commit America still further to a merciless war against Communism in Cuba, Laos, Vietnam or elsewhere. He was assassinated on 22 November 1963.[193]

General Lemnitzer retired from the military in 1969. But in 1975, when the US Senate had begun to examine the exact role of the CIA under the Nixon Administration, he was asked by Gerald Ford, who became the interim President after the Watergate scandal, to take part in the investigation. After he had helped to bury that controversial issue, Ford solicited his help yet again in the running of a pressure group, the Committee on the Present Danger (CPD). This association was a creation of the CIA, then directed by George Bush senior. It led campaigns against the Soviet threat. Among its administrators, one found various CIA officials and Paul D. Wolfowitz (the current Deputy Defense Secretary, in charge of operations in Afghanistan). At the same time, Gerald Ford also promoted Brigadier William H. Craig, who had directed the preliminary studies for the Northwoods operations to director of the National Security Agency (NSA).

General Layman L. Lemnitzer died on 12 November 1988.

In 1992, American public opinion was asking itself questions about the assassination of President Kennedy, following the release of a film by Oliver Stone which showed the incoherence of the official version. President Clinton ordered the declassification of a large number of archives from the Kennedy period. Among the papers of Defense Secretary Robert McNamara was the sole remaining copy of the Northwoods project.

* * *

This historic precedent reminds us than an internal US plot, calling for the sacrifice of American citizens in the context of a terrorist campaign, is, unhappy to say, not impossible. In 1962, John F. Kennedy resisted the lunacy of his military staff. He probably paid for it with his life. We do not know what would have been the reaction of George W. Bush if he faced the same situation.

The most recent history of the United States shows us that domestic terrorism is a growing practice. Since 1996, the FBI publishes an annual report concerning acts of domestic terrorism[194]: four in 1995, eight in 1996, twenty-five in 1997, seventeen in 1998, and nineteen in 1999. Most of them were perpetrated by military and paramilitary groups of the extreme right.

* * *

The existence of a plot within the US armed forces to perpetrate the September 11 attacks is attested to by the deposition of Lieutenant Edward Vreeland before the Superior Court of Toronto (Canada).[195]

Arrested for credit card fraud, Lieutenant Vreeland justified himself by declaring that he worked for US Naval Intelligence. He told policemen that he had gathered information in Russia about the assassination of Marc Bastien, a cipher clerk at the Canadian embassy in Moscow, and about the preparation of attacks in New York. After having verified that Marc Bastien had not been murdered, but died from an overdose of anti-depressants while inebriated, the police dismissed Vreeland's story as merely a pathetic defense. He was jailed.

On 12 August 2001, Vreeland gave a sealed envelope to the penitentiary authorities concerning the coming attacks. The Canadian authorities failed to attach any importance to it. On September 14, they opened the envelope and found a precise description of the attacks

147

committed three days earlier in New York. Making an immediate enquiry to the Pentagon, they were told that Delmart "Mark" Vreeland had left the Navy in 1986, due to his poor performance, and had never been assigned to Naval Intelligence. The Canadian federal prosecutor refused to accept Vreeland's version, exclaiming before the Superior Court of Toronto: *"Is this story possible? I wouldn't go as far as to say it's impossible, only that it's not plausible."*

But in a first twist of events, the coroner, Line Duchesne, reversed himself on the causes of diplomat Marc Bastien's death and concluded that he had been murdered. Vreeland's story recovered its credibility. Then there was a second dramatic development during a public hearing before the Superior Court of Toronto, on 25 January 2002: Lieutenant Vreeland's lawyers, counselors Rocco Galati and Paul Dlansky, using a telephone equipped with a loudspeaker, telephoned the Pentagon switchboard. In the presence of the magistrates listening to the conversation, they obtained confirmation that their client was still on active duty in the Navy. In addition, when they asked to speak to his superiors, the operator put them on a direct line to Naval Intelligence.

* * *

So, here we have attacks that were known beforehand to five intelligence services (German, Egyptian, French, Israeli, and Russian), to a US Naval Intelligence agent such as Vreeland, to the anonymous authors of the warning messages sent to Odigo, not to mention the insider traders who speculated on the stock markets. How far did the leaks go? How far do the implications extend?

Bruce Hoffman, vice-president of the Rand Corporation declared during his hearing before the House of Representatives that, due to their scale, the attacks were "unimaginable".[196]

This was the indisputable verdict of a highly valued expert. With an annual budget of 160 million dollars, the Rand Corporation[197] is the most important private center for research on strategy and military organization in the world. It is the prestigious expression of American military-industrial complex. Presided by James Thomson, it includes among its administrators Ann McLaughlin Korologos (former president of the Aspen Institute) and Frank Carlucci (president of the Carlyle Group). Condoleezza Rice and Donald Rumsfeld were administrators when their official duties permitted it. Zalmay Khalilzad was an analyst there.

But, Bruce Hoffman is not telling the truth: in a speech published by the US Air Force Academy last March (i.e. six months before the attacks), he envisaged precisely the "unimaginable" scenario that took place on September 11.[198] Addressing an audience of Air Force officers, he said that *we try to get our arms around Al-Qaeda, the organization—or maybe the movement—associated with bin Laden. [...] You have to pause here and think for a moment, go back to the bombing of the World Trade Center in 1993 [...] whether it was possible to actually topple the north tower onto the south tower and kill 60,000 people [...] They are not going to lay down their arms and give up, so they will find other weapons and tactics and means to reach their targets. And here is an obvious class of weapon choices: ultralights, UAVs* [i.e. remote controlled planes], *all types of distance and stand-off weapons.*"

What foresight, *n'est-ce pas*?

* * *

In order to calm the bellicose ardors of the Republican Party, during the vote for the annual budget in 2000, the Democrats accepted the creation of a commission to evaluate the organization and the planning of United States security in outer space. The commission published its report[199] on 11 January 2001, a few days before its chairman, the honorable Donald Rumsfeld, was to become Defense Secretary in the Bush Administration, and left his seat on the board of directors at the Rand Corporation. Eight of the Commission's twelve members were retired generals. All of them were advocates for an "*anti-missile shield*", so that the thirty-two days of the commission's deliberations were not spent preparing an audit of the situation, but in looking for arguments that would justify *a posteriori* the shared convictions of its members.

For the "*Rumsfeld Commission*", space is a military domain comparable to the land, sea and air. It should therefore have its own service arm, equivalent to the Army, Navy, or Air Force. The United States should occupy this domain and prevent any other power from installing itself there. Thanks to this asymmetry of means, U.S. military supremacy will be uncontestable and unlimited.

The Rumsfeld Commission listed ten proposals:

1 – The Space Force should be placed directly under the President's orders.

2 – The President should create a national councilor for space issues so that United States might better exploit its advantage.

3 – The various intelligence agencies should be coordinated and subordinated to the Space Force within the National Security Council.

4 – The Space Force would be both an intelligence tool and a lethal armed force, its use supposing the coordination of the Defense Secretary and the numerous intelligence services; the latter being placed under the sole authority of the CIA director.

5 – The Secretary of Defense should be assisted by an Under-Secretary for space affairs.

6 – The Space Force command should be distinct from that of the Air Force.

7 – The Space Force should be able to dispose of the other armed services.

8 – The NRO (the agency in charge of remote imaging from space) should be attached to the Under-Secretary for Space;

9 – The Secretary of Defense should directly supervise investments in research & development of space, in such a way to increase the asymmetry between U.S. forces and those of other military powers.

10 – Very important budgetary means should be released for the space military program.

Other than the fact that it requires the termination of the 1972 ABM Treaty, this ambitious program for the militarization of space supposes such reforms in American organization and strategy that it seems unrealizable. That is why the Rumsfeld Commission wrote:

"History is replete with instances in which warning signs were ignored and change resisted until an external, 'improbable' event forced resistant bureaucra-

cies to take action. The question is whether the U.S. will be wise enough to act responsibly and soon enough to reduce U.S. space vulnerability. Or whether, as in the past, a disabling attack against the country and its people – a 'Space Pearl Harbor' – will be the only event able to galvanize the nation and cause the U.S. Government to act. We are on notice, but we have not noticed.

For Donald Rumsfeld and the Air Force generals, the events of September 11 constituted a kind of *"divine surprise"*, to use the expression employed by French fascists when France's defeat in 1940 permitted them to overthrow *"the Wretch"* (i.e. the French Third Republic) and entrust Philippe Pétain with emergency powers.

On September 11, at 6:42 pm, Donald Rumsfeld held a press conference at the Pëntagon.[200] To demonstrate the unity of America in that difficult hour, the Democratic and Republican leaders of the Senate Armed Services Commission joined him. There was no news of President Bush and the world anxiously awaited the US. Right there in the middle of the press conference, live before the cameras of the international press, Donald Rumsfeld scolded Senator Carl Levin (D – Michigan): *"Senator Levin, you and other Democrats in Congress have voiced fear that you simply don't have enough money for the large increase in defense that the Pentagon is seeking, especially for missile defense, and you fear that you'll have to dip into the Social Security funds to pay for it. Does this sort of thing convince you that an emergency exists in this country to increase defense spending, to dip into Social Security, if necessary, to pay for defense spending – increase defense spending?"*

Such heated words might be construed as a confession.

EPILOGUE

If the energy lobby is the first beneficiary of the war in Afghanistan, the military-industrial lobby was the great victor of September 11. Its wildest hopes will henceforth be fulfilled.

Before all else, the ABM Treaty, fixing limits to weapons development, was denounced by George W. Bush.

Next, not only was the director of the CIA not dismissed after its apparent failure on September 11, but the agency's funding was immediately increased by 42% to successfully carry out the "*Worldwide Attack Matrix*".

The military budget of the United States, which had been steadily reduced since the dissolution of the USSR, has undergone a sudden, vertiginous increase. If one adds up all the supplementary funds hastily voted in the wake of the attacks and the budget increases planned since, the first two years of the Bush presidency will see a rise of 24% in military spending. Over five years, the budget of the U.S. armed forces will represent more than two trillion dollars, although the arms race is over and there is no major enemy at hand. The U.S. military budget is now equal to the combined total for the twenty-five next biggest armies in the world.

The areas receiving the lion's share of this budget increase concern space and secret operations, demonstrating the predominance within the American state apparatus of the alliance between the heads of those secret operations (grouped around George Tenet) and the advocates of the Space Force. The latter are grouped around Donald Rumsfeld and General Ralph E. Eberhart, the current commander-in-chief of NORAD and the principal superior officer directing air traffic control operations on 11 September 2001.

The course taken by the American Administration with the events of September 11, seem to announce plenty of *"blood, sweat and tears"*, to use Winston Churchill's phrase. It remains now to be seen who on this planet will bear the costs.

February 2002.

DOCUMENTS & APPENDICES

THE MILITARY BUDGETS
OF MAJOR COUNTRIES

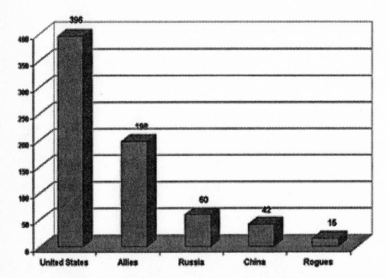

Source: http://www.cdi.org/issues/wme

The two tables (in billions of U.S. dollars) show the overwhelming weight of American military spending, greater than that of the total of the following twenty-five countries.

(*) "Allies" include the countries of NATO, Australia, Japan, and South Korea. "Rogues" group together Cuba, Iran, Iraq, Libya, North Korea, Sudan, and Syria.

United States	**396**
Russia	60
China	42
Japoan	40
United Kingdom	34
Saoudi Arabia	27
France	25
Germany	21
Brazil	17
India	15
Italy	15
South Korea	11
Iran	9
Israel	9
Taiwan	8
Canada	7
Spain	6
Australia	6
Netherlands	5
Turkey	5
Singapore	4
Sweden	4
Unit. Arab Emirates	3
Poland	3
Greece	3
Argentina	3
Total excluding US	**382**

(in billions US dollars)

AMERICA'S HOLY WAR

by William S. Cohen

As of 12 September 2001, the day after the attacks, the former Secretary of Defense under Bill Clinton, William S. Cohen, called for the replacement of the ideology of the "Cold War against Communism" by the "war against terrorism" in an opinion piece with the evocative title: *America's Holy War*.[201] This guest editorial, published in the *Washington Post*, prefigured the political and religious rhetoric of the crusade that George W. Bush was about to launch.

As the smoke clears from the skies of New York, Washington and western Pennsylvania, much remains unknown this morning regarding yesterday's terrorist attacks. But what is certain is that the American people will not succumb to terrorists — and will not rest until justice is done to those responsible.

As a free society, and one that is constantly renewed and strengthened by integrating individuals from all lands and cultures, America is particularly vulnerable to those who exploit our openness. The objective of such terrorists is to cause America to cower — to withdraw from the world and to abandon our ideals. But America cannot wrap itself in a continental cocoon, safely isolated from a troubled world. We have global economic, political and security interests that require our active involvement abroad. Even if we did retreat, America would remain such a potent symbol that those lashing out over perceived grievances would still aim their wrath at the United States.

Too many generations have paid the ultimate price defending our freedom for us to retreat from the world or retrench from our values. In a very real sense, America itself must embark on its own holy war — not one driven by hatred or fueled by blood but grounded in our commitment to freedom, tolerance and the rule of law and buttressed by our willingness to use all means available to defend these values. Just as those who pursue terror have been relentless in their efforts, so must we be in ours.

No government can guarantee the full safety of its citizens either abroad or at home. But no government can permit its citizens to be attacked with impunity if it hopes to retain the loyalty and confidence of those it is charged to protect.

(...)

To be effective, this effort will require greater international cooperation, intelligence collection abroad, and information gathering by law enforcement agencies at home. Information is power, and greater access to information will require the American people and their elected officials to find the proper balance between privacy and protection. It has been difficult to get sustained, thoughtful, broad-based dialogue on this delicate topic, but the sooner such dialogue occurs the more likely it is we will strike the right balance. This will raise difficult questions regarding government intrusion, but the main threat to our civil liberties stems from the chaos and carnage that could result from a biological attack for which we were insufficiently prepared and the demands for action that would follow. Those who engage in terror feed on any display of fear or weakness, and those attacked must either fight or fold. Our people, not just our government, stood up to the fascist and then the communist threat to freedom. Americans did not triumph in the long, twilight struggle of the Cold War only to forfeit our victory to anonymous extremists in this war. As with the last, this struggle will not be won with a single military response. Victory will require the American people to display courage, faith, unity and determination to carry on for the indefinite future.

SENATE CONFIRMATION HEARING: GENERAL MYERS

General Richard Myers appeared before the Armed Services Commission of the United States Senate on 13 September 2001. This hearing, scheduled for some time, had as its object confirmation of the general's appointment to the post of Chairman of the Joint Chiefs of Staff, in replacement of General Hugh Shelton. In light of events two days earlier, the hearing also concerned the military response to the attacks.

General Myers was in the office of Senator Cleland at the time of the attack. He only arrived at the Pentagon after some delay, and then conducted operations from the National Military Command Center, in his role as Deputy Chairman of the Joint Chiefs of Staff, General Shelton being away in Brussels.

In his declarations before the Commission, General Myers revealed himself incapable of describing the military response to the attacks, giving the impression that no response had been made. To complete or correct this impression, NORAD later issued a press release attesting that fighters had attempted to intercept the three planes deviated towards New York or Washington.

Senator Carl Levin: *Was the Defense Department contacted by the FAA or the FBI or any other agency after the first two hijacked aircraft crashed into the World Trade Center, prior to the time the Pentagon was hit?*

General Richard Myers: *Sir, I don't know the answer to that question. I can get that for you, for the record.*

Levin: *Thank you. Did the Defense Department take – or was the Defense Department asked to take action against any specific aircraft?*

Myers: *Sir, we were...*

Levin: *And did you take action against – for instance, there have been statements that the aircraft that crashed in Pennsylvania was shot down. Those stories continue to exist.*

Myers: *Mr. Chairman, the armed forces did not shoot down any aircraft. When it became clear what the threat was, we did scramble fighter aircraft, AWACS, radar aircraft and tanker aircraft to begin to establish orbits in case other aircraft showed up in the FAA system that were hijacked. But we never actually had to use force.*

Levin: *Was that order that you just described given before or after the Pentagon was struck?*

Myers: *That order, to the best of my knowledge, was after the Pentagon was struck.*

(...)

Senator Bill Nelson: *Mr. Chairman, may I, just for the record? Commenting from CNN on the timeline, 9:03 is the correct time that the United Airlines flight crashed into the south tower of the World Trade Center; 9:43 is the time that American Airlines flight 77 crashed into the Pentagon. And 10:10 a.m. is the time that United Airlines flight 93 crashed in Somerset County, Pennsylvania.*

So that was 40 minutes between the second tower being hit and the Pentagon crash. And it is an hour and seven minutes until the crash occurred in Pennsylvania.

Levin: *The time that we don't have is when the Pentagon was notified, if they were, by the FAA or the FBI or any other agency, relative to any potential threat or any planes having changed direction or anything like that. And that's the same which you will give us because that's...*

Myers: *I can answer that. At the time of the first impact on the World Trade Center, we stood up our crisis action team. That was done immediately.*

So we stood it up. And we started talking to the federal agencies. The time I do not know is when NORAD responded with fighter aircraft. I don't know that time

Levin: *Or the time that I asked you for, which was whether the FAA or FBI notified you that other planes had turned direction from their path, their scheduled path, and were returning or aiming towards Washington, whether there was any notice from any of them, because that's such an obvious shortfall if there wasn't.*

Myers: *Right.*

Levin: *And in any event, but more important, if you get us that information.*

Myers: *It probably happened. As you remember, I was not in the Pentagon at that time, so that part of it is a little hazy. After that, we started getting regular notifications through NORAD, FAA to NORAD, on other flights that we were worried about.*

And we knew about the one that eventually crashed in Pennsylvania. I do not know, again, whether we had fighters scrambled on it. I have to...

Levin: *If you could get us those times then. We know you don't know them.*

Myers: *But we'll get them.*

INTERVIEW WITH
VICE PRESIDENT CHENEY

Invited to take part in the television program, *Meet the Press* (NBC)[202], Vice President Cheney recounted before television views the manner in which he experienced the events of September 11. One will observe that the Secret Service exercised authority over a key elected political leader. One notes as well the incredible episode of the plane circling over Washington without any intervention from anti-aircraft defenses.

Vice President Cheney: *While I was there* [at his office in the West Wing of the White House], *over the next several minutes, watching developments on television and as we started to get organized to figure out what to do, my Secret Service agents came in and, under these circumstances, they just move. They don't say "sir" or ask politely. They came in and said, "Sir, we have to leave immediately," and grabbed me and...*

Tim Russert: *Literally grabbed you and moved you?*

Vice President Cheney: *Yeah. And, you know, your feet touch the floor periodically. But they're bigger than I am, and they hoisted me up and moved me very rapidly down the hallway, down some stairs, through some doors and down some more stairs into an underground facility under the White House, and, as a matter of fact, it's a corridor, locked at both ends, and they did that because they had received a report that an airplane was headed for the White House.*

Tim Russert: *This is Flight 77, which had left Dulles.*

Vice President Cheney: *Which turned out to be Flight 77. It left Dulles, flown west towards Ohio, been captured by the terrorists. They turned off the transponder, which led to a later report that a plane had gone down over Ohio, but it really hadn't. Of course, then they turned back and headed back towards Washington. As best we can tell, they came initially at the White House and...*

Tim Russert: *The plane actually circled the White House?*

Vice President Cheney: *Didn't circle it, but was headed on a track into it. The Secret Service has an arrangement with the FAA. They had open lines after the World Trade Center was...*

Tim Russert: *Tracking it by radar.*

Vice President Cheney: *And when it entered the danger zone and looked like it was headed for the White House was when they grabbed me and evacuated me to the basement. The plane obviously didn't hit the White House. It turned away and, we think, flew a circle and came back in and then hit the Pentagon. And that's what the radar track looks like.*

(...)

Vice President Cheney: *The president was on Air Force One. We received a threat to Air Force One – came through the Secret Service...*

Tim Russert: *A credible threat to Air Force One? You're convinced of that?*

Vice President Cheney: *I'm convinced of that. Now, you know, it may have been phoned in by a crank, but in the midst of what was going on, there was no way to know that. I think it was a credible threat, enough for the Secret Service to bring it to me. Once I left that immediate shelter, after I talked to the president, urged him to stay away for now, well, I went down into what's called a PEOC, the Presidential Emergency Operations Center, and there I had Norm Mineta, secretary of Transportation, access to the FAA (...)*

STATE SPONSORS OF TERRORISM
SHOULD BE WIPED OUT, TOO

by Richard Perle

In a guest editorial published in London by the *Daily Telegraph*[203] on 18 September 2001, one of the Washington "hawks", Richard Perle, denounced the lack of combativeness on the part of U.S. allies. He perceived a sort of "Vichyism" in the overly precise questioning of the identity of the terrorists, and refused in advance the choice of certain alliances. In his eyes, some states need to be eliminated, regardless of whether or not they were implicated in the attacks or were opposed themselves to Osama bin Laden and the Taliban. Here, the epithet of "terrorist" does not designate groups having recourse to a form of military action, but instead stigmatizes the enemies of the United States. Former Deputy Secretary of Defense under Ronald Reagan (1981-1987) Richard Perle is a collaborator of the Center for Security Policy and an editor for the *Jerusalem Post*.

There is an air of Vichyite defeatism about some of the commentary in Britain on the current war on terrorism.

We constantly hear the reiteration of such themes as "We don't know who the enemy is", "We don't know where to strike them", "Even if we could find them, it would simply create more martyrs" and that "The Wret-

ched of the Earth" (to use the title of Franz Fanon's famous anti-colonial tract) are so desperate that they would not fear honourable death at the hands of what they see as the "Great Satan".

The US Defence Secretary, Donald Rumsfeld, and other senior Administration officials are quite right to say that it is a totally new kind of war which the Free World now faces. But even though it is new, the Vichyite contingent would be quite wrong to extrapolate from that that the US and its allies are impotent.

Even if we don't yet know the whole story about last week's atrocities, we know enough to act, and to act decisively. The truth is that the international community has not created a new world order in which sponsorship of terrorism by states is beyond the pale. Without the things that only states can provide – sanctuary, intelligence, logistics, training, communications, money – even the bin Laden network and others like it could manage only the occasional car bomb. Deprive the terrorists of the offices from which they now work, remove the vast infrastructure now supporting them and force them to sleep in a different place every night because they are hunted - and the scope of their activity will be sharply reduced.

(...)

Iran has its own reasons for supporting military action against the Taliban regime in Afghanistan. But no one should confuse Iranian support for such action with an Iranian commitment to oppose terrorism. It is unthinkable that we could admit them into the coalition. An anti-terrorist coalition that has any reasonable prospect of success will be made up of countries that value democratic institutions, individual liberty and the sanctity of life.

It cannot include countries who repress their own

people, violate fundamental human rights and scorn the fundamental values of western civilisation. Momentary, fleeting collaboration for immediate tactical advantage may make sense, as Churchill understood in joining with the Soviet Union to defeat Nazism. No coalition to defeat terrorism can include countries that countenance campaigns of hate and vilification. Countries that tolerate the incitement to kill civilians - Americans, Britons, Israelis and others - have no legitimate role in the war against terrorism.

Some countries may be unwilling or unable to participate in a coalition that demands a respect for the values and norms of western civilisation. The nature of their hold on power may be inconsistent with genuine opposition to terrorism. Such countries are part of the problem, not the solution, and we neither need their help nor would benefit from their professions of support.

Those countries that harbour terrorists – that provide the means with which they would destroy innocent civilians must themselves be destroyed. The war against terrorism is about the war against those regimes. We will not win the war against terror by chasing individual terrorists, any more than we will win the war against drugs by arresting the "mules" who pass through Heathrow. It is the networks that send young men on suicide missions and their sponsors that must be destroyed.

A NEW KIND OF WAR

by Donald Rumsfeld

This guest editorial from the Secretary of Defense appeared in the *New York Times* on 27 September 2001.[204]
In the type of war presented, the notions of "civilian" and "military" vanish in favor of a society in which each individual, whoever he or she may be, is liable to be impressed to fight, according to the concept of "total war" defined by Goebbels.

President Bush is rallying the nation for a war against terrorism's attack on our way of life. Some believe the first casualty of any war is the truth. But in this war, the first victory must be to tell the truth. And the truth is, this will be a war like none other our nation has faced. Indeed, it is easier to describe what lies ahead by talking about what it is not rather than what it is.

This war will not be waged by a grand alliance united for the single purpose of defeating an axis of hostile powers. Instead, it will involve floating coalitions of countries, which may change and evolve. Countries will have different roles and contribute in different ways. Some will provide diplomatic support, others financial, still others logistical or military. Some will help us publicly, while others, because of their circumstances, may help us privately and secretly. In this war, the mission will define the coalition — not the other way around.

We understand that countries we consider our friends may help with certain efforts or be silent on others, while other actions we take may depend on the involvement of countries we have considered less than friendly.

In this context, the decision by the United Arab Emirates and Saudi Arabia — friends of the United States — to break ties with the Taliban is an important early success of this campaign, but should not suggest they will be a part of every action we may contemplate.

This war will not necessarily be one in which we pore over military targets and mass forces to seize those targets. Instead, military force will likely be one of many tools we use to stop individuals, groups and countries that engage in terrorism.

Our response may include firing cruise missiles into military targets somewhere in the world; we are just as likely to engage in electronic combat to track and stop investments moving through offshore banking centers. The uniforms of this conflict will be bankers' pinstripes and programmers' grunge just as assuredly as desert camouflage.[205]

This is not a war against an individual, a group, a religion or a country. Rather, our opponent is a global network of terrorist organizations and their state sponsors, committed to denying free people the opportunity to live as they choose. While we may engage militarily against foreign governments that sponsor terrorism, we may also seek to make allies of the people those governments suppress.

Even the vocabulary of this war will be different. When we "invade the enemy's territory," we may well be invading his cyberspace. There may not be as many bea-

chheads stormed as opportunities denied. Forget about "exit strategies"; we're looking at a sustained engagement that carries no deadlines. We have no fixed rules about how to deploy our troops; we'll instead establish guidelines to determine whether military force is the best way to achieve a given objective.

The public may see some dramatic military engagements that produce no apparent victory, or may be unaware of other actions that lead to major victories. "Battles" will be fought by customs officers stopping suspicious persons at our borders and diplomats securing cooperation against money laundering.

But if this is a different kind of war, one thing is unchanged: America remains indomitable. Our victory will come with Americans living their lives day by day, going to work, raising their children and building their dreams as they always have – a free and great people.

THE WHITE HOUSE

WASHINGTON

October 5, 2001

MEMORANDUM FOR THE SECRETARY OF STATE
THE SECRETARY OF THE TREASURY
THE SECRETARY OF DEFENSE
THE ATTORNEY GENERAL
THE DIRECTOR OF CENTRAL INTELLIGENCE
THE DIRECTOR OF FEDERAL BUREAU OF INVESTIGATION

SUBJECT: Disclosures to the Congress

As we wage our campaign to respond to the terrorist attacks against the United States on September 11, and to protect us from further acts of terrorism, I intend to continue to work closely with the Congress. Consistent with longstanding executive branch practice, this Administration will continue to work to inform the leadership of the Congress about the course of, and important developments in, our critical military, intelligence, and law enforcement operations. At the same time, we have an obligation to protect military operational security, intelligence sources and methods, and sensitive law enforcement investigations. Accordingly, your departments should adhere to the following procedures when providing briefings to the Congress relating to the information we have or the actions we plan to take:

(i)   Only you or officers expressly designated by you may brief Members of Congress regarding classified or sensitive law enforcement information; and

(ii) The only Members of Congress whom you or your expressly designated officers may brief regarding classified or sensitive law enforcement information are the Speaker of the House, the House Minority Leader, the Senate Majority and Minority Leaders, and the Chairs and Ranking Members of the Intelligence Committees in the House and Senate.

This approach will best serve our shared goals of protecting American lives, maintaining the proper level of confidentiality for the success of our military, intelligence, and law enforcement operations, and keeping the leadership of the Congress appropriately informed about important developments. This morning, I informed the House and Senate leadership of this policy which shall remain in effect until you receive further notice from me.

DEPUTY SECRETARY OF DEFENSE
1010 DEFENSE PENTAGON
WASHINGTON, DC 20301-1010

1 8 OCT 2001

MEMORANDUM FOR SECRETARIES OF THE MILITARY DEPARTMENTS
CHAIRMAN OF THE JOINT CHIEFS OF STAFF
UNDER SECRETARIES OF DEFENSE
DIRECTOR, DEFENSE RESEARCH AND ENGINEERING
ASSISTANT SECRETARIES OF DEFENSE
GENERAL COUNSEL OF THE DEPARTMENT OF DEFENSE
INSPECTOR GENERAL OF THE DEPARTMENT OF DEFENSE
DIRECTOR, OPERATIONAL TEST AND EVALUATION
ASSISTANTS TO THE SECRETARY OF DEFENSE
DIRECTOR, NET ASSESSMENT
DIRECTORS OF THE DEFENSE AGENCIES
DIRECTOR OF THE DOD FIELD ACTIVITIES

SUBJECT: Operations Security Throughout the Department of Defense

On 14 September the President declared a national emergency by reason of terrorist attacks and the continuing and immediate threat of further attacks on the United States. As this Department assists wide-ranging efforts to defeat international terrorism, it is clear that US military and civilian service lives, DOD operational capabilities, facilities and resources, and the security of information critical to the national security will remain at risk for an indefinite period.

It is therefore vital that Defense Department employees, as well as persons in other organizations that support DOD, exercise *great* caution in discussing information related to DOD work, regardless of their duties. Do not conduct *any* work-related conversations in common areas, public places, while commuting, or over unsecured electronic circuits. Classified information may be discussed *only* in authorized spaces and with persons having a specific need to know and the proper security clearance. Unclassified information may likewise require protection because it can often be compiled to reveal sensitive conclusions. Much of the information we use to conduct DOD's operations must be withheld from public release because of its sensitivity. If in doubt, do not release or discuss official information except with other DoD personnel.

All major components in this Department to include the Office of the Secretary of Defense, the Military Departments, the Joint Staff, the Combatant Commands, the Defense Agencies, the DOD Field Activities and all other organizational entities within the DOD will review the Operations Security (OPSEC) Program, described in DOD Directive 5205.2, and ensure that their policies, procedures and personnel are in compliance. We must ensure that we deny our adversaries the information essential for them to plan, prepare or conduct further terrorist or related hostile operations against the United States and this Department.

Paul Wolfowitz

SPEECH BY LAURA BUSH TO THE NATION

On 17 November 2001, the wife of George W. Bush, Laura, addressed the nation in a message broadcast on radio. According to the First Lady, the objective of the military campaign in Afghanistan was not the construction of a pipeline, but rather the defense of the rights of Afghan women and children.

Good morning.
I'm Laura Bush, and I'm delivering this week's radio address to kick off a world-wide effort to focus on the brutality against women and children by the al-Qaeda terrorist network and the regime it supports in Afghanistan, the Taliban. That regime is now in retreat across much of the country, and the people of Afghanistan – especially women – are rejoicing. Afghan women know, through hard experience, what the rest of the world is discovering: the brutal oppression of women is a central goal of the terrorists. Long before the current war began, the Taliban and its terrorist allies were making the lives of children and women in Afghanistan miserable. Seventy percent of the Afghan people are malnourished. One in every four children won't live past the age of five because health care is not available. Women have been denied access to doctors when they're sick. Life under the Taliban is so hard and repressive, even small displays of joy are outlawed – children aren't allowed to fly kites; their mothers face beatings for laughing

out loud. Women cannot work outside the home, or even leave their homes by themselves.

The severe repression and brutality against women in Afghanistan is not a matter of legitimate religious practice. Muslims around the world have condemned the brutal degradation of women and children by the Taliban regime. The poverty, poor health, and illiteracy that the terrorists and the Taliban have imposed on women in Afghanistan do not conform with the treatment of women in most of the Islamic world, where women make important contributions in their societies. Only the terrorists and the Taliban forbid education to women. Only the terrorists and the Taliban threaten to pull out women's fingernails for wearing nail polish. The plight of women and children in Afghanistan is a matter of deliberate human cruelty, carried out by those who seek to intimidate and control.

Civilized people throughout the world are speaking out in horror – not only because our hearts break for the women and children in Afghanistan, but also because in Afghanistan, we see the world the terrorists would like to impose on the rest of us.

All of us have an obligation to speak out. We may come from different backgrounds and faiths – but parents the world over love our children. We respect our mothers, our sisters and daughters. Fighting brutality against women and children is not the expression of a specific culture; it is the acceptance of our common humanity – a commitment shared by people of good will on every continent. Because of our recent military gains in much of Afghanistan, women are no longer imprisoned in their homes. They can listen to music and teach their daughters without fear of punishment. Yet the ter-

rorists who helped rule that country now plot and plan in many countries. And they must be stopped. The fight against terrorism is also a fight for the rights and dignity of women.

In America, next week brings Thanksgiving. After the events of the last few months, we'll be holding our families even closer. And we will be especially thankful for all the blessings of American life. I hope Americans will join our family in working to insure that dignity and opportunity will be secured for all the women and children of Afghanistan.

Have a wonderful holiday, and thank you for listening.

Laura Bush addressing the Nation
Source: White House:
http://www.whitehouse.gov/news/releases/2001/11/images/
20011117-2.html

MARTIAL JUSTICE, FULL AND FAIR

by Alberto Gonzales

In a guest editorial published on 30 November 2001 in the *New York Times*[206], Alberto Gonzales, legal counsel to George W. Bush, defended the Presidential Order (drafted by Gonzales himself) creating the military commissions for captured foreign terrorist suspects.

Like presidents before him, President Bush has invoked his power to establish military commissions to try enemy belligerents who commit war crimes. In appropriate circumstances, these commissions provide important advantages over civilian trials. They spare American jurors, judges and courts the grave risks associated with terrorist trials. They allow the government to use classified information as evidence without compromising intelligence or military efforts. They can dispense justice swiftly, close to where our forces may be fighting, without years of pretrial proceedings or post-trial appeals.

And they can consider the broadest range of relevant evidence to reach their verdicts. For example, circumstances in a war zone often make it impossible to meet the authentication requirements for documents in a civilian court, yet documents from Al Qaeda safe houses in Kabul might be essential to accurately determine the guilt of Qaeda cell members hiding in the West.

Some in Congress and some civil libertarians remain skeptical of the military commissions. Their criticism, while well-intentioned, is wrong and is based on misconceptions about what the president's order does and how it will function.

The order covers only foreign enemy war criminals; it does not cover United States citizens or even enemy soldiers abiding by the laws of war. Under the order, the president will refer to military commissions only non-citizens who are members or active supporters of Al Qaeda or other international terrorist organizations targeting the United States. The president must determine that it would be in the interests of the United States that these people be tried by military commission, and they must be chargeable with offenses against the international laws of war, like targeting civilians or hiding in civilian populations and refusing to bear arms openly. Enemy war criminals are not entitled to the same procedural protections as people who violate our domestic laws.

Military commission trials are not secret. The president's order authorizes the secretary of defense to close proceedings to protect classified information. It does not require that any trial, or even portions of a trial, be conducted in secret. Trials before military commissions will be as open as possible, consistent with the urgent needs of national security. The specter of mass secret trials, as depicted by critics, is not an accurate reflection of the order or the president's intent.

The order specifically directs that all trials before military commissions will be "full and fair". Everyone tried before a military commission will know the charges against him, be represented by qualified counsel and be *allowed to present a defense. The American military justice system is the finest in the world, with longstanding traditions of forbidding command influence on proceedings, of providing zealous advocacy by competent defense counsel, and of procedural fairness. Military commissions employed during World War II even acquitted some German and Japanese defendants. The suggestion that these commissions will afford only sham justice like that dispensed in dictatorial nations is an insult to our military justice system.*

The order preserves judicial review in civilian courts. Under the order, anyone arrested, detained or tried in the United States by a military commission will be able to challenge the lawfulness of the commission's jurisdiction through a habeas corpus proceeding in a federal court. The language of the order is similar to the language of a military tribunal order issued by President Franklin Roosevelt that was construed by the Supreme Court to permit habeas corpus review.

Military commissions are consistent with American historical and constitutional traditions. Confederate agents disguised as civilians traveling to New York to set it afire were tried by military commission. Nazi saboteurs who came ashore on Long Island during World War II disguised as civilians and intending to attack American war industries were tried before military commissions. The use of such commissions has been consistently upheld by the Supreme Court.

Military commissions do not undermine the constitutional values of civil liberties or separation of powers; they protect them by ensuring that the United States may wage war against external enemies and defeat them. To defend the nation, President Bush has rightly sought to employ every lawful means at his disposal. Military commissions are one such means, and their judicious use will help keep Americans safe and free.

THE LIST OF THE NINETEEN KAMIKAZES PUBLISHED BY THE FBI

American Airlines Flight 11
(crashed into the north tower of the World Trade Center)

1) Satam M.A. Alsuqami
Probably a Saudi citizen;
Date of birth used: 28 June 1976
Last known address: United Arab Emirates...
2) Waleed M. Alshehri
Probably a Saudi citizen;
Dates of birth used: 13 September 1974, 3 March 1976, 8 July 1977, 20 December 1978,
11 May 1979, 5 November 1979;
Domiciled in Hollywood, Florida; Orlando, Florida; and Daytona Beach, Florida;
Alleged airplane pilot.
3) Wail M. Alshehri
Date of birth used: 1 September 1968;
Domiciled in Hollywood, Florida and Newton, Massachusetts;
Alleged airplane pilot.
4) Mohamed Atta
Probably an Egyptian citizen;
Date of birth used: 1 September, 1968;
Domiciled in Hollywood, Florida; Coral Springs, Florida; and Hamburg, Germany;

Alleged airplane pilot;
Aliases: Mehan Atta, Mohammad El Amir, Muhammad Atta, Mohamed El Sayed, Mohamed Elsayed, Muhammad Muhammad Al Amir Awag Al Sayyid Atta, Muhammad Muhammad Al- Amir Awad Al Sayad.

5) Abdulazis Alomari
Probably a Saudi citizen;
Dates of birth used: 24 December 1972 and 28 May 1979;
Domiciled in Hollywood, Florida;
Alleged airplane pilot.

United Airlines Flight 175
(crashed into the south tower of the World Trade Center)

1) Marwan Al-Shehhi
Date of birth used: 9 May 1979;
Domiciled in Hollywood, Florida;
Alleged airplane pilot;
Aliases: Marwan Yusif Muhammad Rashid Al-Shehi, Marwan Yusif Muhammad Rashid Lakrab Al-Shihhi, Abu Abdullah.

2) Fayez Rashid Ahmed Hassan Al Qadi Banihammad
Domiciled in Delray Beach, Florida;
Aliases: Fayez Ahmad, Banihammad Fayez Abu Dhabi Banihammad, Fayez Rashid Ahmed, Banihammad Fayez, Rasid Ahmed Hassen Alqadi, Abu Dhabi Banihammad, Ahmed Fayez, Faez Ahmed.

3) Ahmed Alghamdi
Alias: Ahmed Salah Alghamdi.

4) Hamza Alghamdi
Domiciled in Delray Beach, Florida;
Aliases: Hamza Al-Ghamdi, Hamza Ghamdi, Hamzah Alghamdi, Hamza Alghamdi Saleh.
5) Mohand Alshehri
Domiciled in Delray Beach, Florida;
Aliases: Mohammed Alshehhi, Mahamd Alshehri, Mohald Alshehri.

American Airlines Flight 77
(crashed into Pentagon)

1) Khalid Almihdhar
Probably a Saudi citizen;
Domiciled in San Diego, California and New York;
Aliases: Sannan Al-Makki, Khalid Bin Muhammad, Addallah Al-Mihdhar, Khalid Mohammad Al-Saqaf
2) Majed Moqed
Probably a Saudi citizen;
Aliases: Majed M.GH Moqed, Majed Moqed, Majed Mashaan Moqed.
3) Nawaf Alhazmi
Probably a Saudi citizen;
Domiciled in Fort Lee, New Jersey; Wayne, New Jersey; and San Diego, California;
Aliases: Nawaf Al-Hazmi, Nawaf Al Hazmi, Nawaf M.S. Al Hazmi.
4) Salem Alhazmi
Probably a Saudi citizen;
Domiciled in Fort Lee, New Jersey and Wayne, New Jersey.

5) Hani Hanjour
Domiciled in Phoenix, Arizona and San Diego, California;
Aliases: Hani Saleh Hanjour, Hani Saleh, Hani Hanjour, Hani Saleh H. Hanjour.

United Airlines Flight 93
(exploded in flight over Stony Creek Township, Pennsylvania)

1) Saeed Alghamdi
Domiciled in Delray Beach, Florida;
Aliases: Abdul Rahman Saed Alghamdi, Ali S. Alghamdi, Al- Ghamdi, Saad M.S. Al Ghamdi, Sadda Al Ghamdi, Saheed Al-Ghamdi, Seed Al Ghamdi.
2) Ahmed Ibrahim A. Al Haznawi
Probably a Saudi citizen;
Date of birth used: 11 October 1980;
Domiciled in Delray Beach, Florida;
Alias: Ahmed Alhaznawi.
3) Ahmed Alnami
Domiciled in Delray Beach, Florida;
Alias: Ali Ahmed Alnami, Ahmed A. Al-Nami, Ahmed Al- Nawi.
4) Ziad Samir Jarrah
Alleged airplane pilot;
Aliases: Zaid Jarrahi, Zaid Samr Jarrah, Ziad S. Jarrah, Ziad Jarrah Jarrat, Ziad Sami Jarrahi.

TRANSCRIPT OF A VIDEO CASSETTE
OF OSAMA BIN LADEN
PUBLISHED BY THE US DEPARTMENT
OF DEFENSE AND
THE US STATE DEPARTMENT

Preliminary note from the State Department

The Defense Department has released a videotape of al-Qaeda leader Osama bin Laden discussing the September 11 terrorist attacks against the World Trade Center and the Pentagon during a courtesy visit with an unidentified Sheikh that is believed to have taken place in the southern Afghan city of Kandahar in mid-November.

The tape and the transcript of an English translation of the tape were released in Washington on December 13. Segments of the transcript are not verbatim. The tape, of poor quality, shows Bin Laden saying that the devastation caused by the fuel-laden jetliners crashing into the twin towers of the trade center far exceeded his expectations.

"We calculated in advance the number of casualties from the enemy, who would be killed based on the position of the tower. We calculated that the floors that would be hit would be three or four floors. I was the most optimistic of them all. (...Inaudible...) due to my experience in this field, I was thinking that the fire from the gas in the plane would melt the iron structure of the building and collapse the area where the plane hit and all the floors above it only. This is all that we had hoped for," Bin Laden said.

The Sheikh whom Bin Laden was visiting answered, *"Allah be praised."*

Elsewhere in the tape, Bin Laden said the al-Qaeda terrorists who carried out the attacks were informed that they were on a *"martyrdom operation"* when they were sent to the United States, but they did not receive instructions about the details of the operation until just before they boarded the airplanes on September 11. Bin Laden said the pilots among the hijackers and the other groups of terrorists did not know each other.

The Defense Department, in a December 13 news release, said the videotape was discovered by U.S. forces in Jalalabad, Afghanistan in late November. In a question and answer document dealing with the tape, the Defense Department said the way the tape was obtained suggests that it was left behind by someone who was departing in a rush, but it is also possible that the tape was left behind intentionally.

Translations and transcriptions of the tape were provided by private, independent translators. The private translations were compared with translations done by the U.S. government and no inconsistencies were found, the Defense Department said.

Following is the transcript of the English translation:

Transcript of Osama bin Laden Video Tape

Transcript and annotations prepared by private, independent contractors. They collaborated on the translation and compared it with one done by the U.S. Government for consistency.

In mid-November, Osama Bin Laden spoke to a

room of supporters, possibly in Kandahar, Afghanistan. These comments were video taped with the knowledge of Bin Laden and all present.

Note: The tape is approximately one hour long and contains three different segments: an original taping of a visit by some people to the site of the downed U.S. helicopter in Ghazni province (approximately 12 minutes long); and two segments documenting a courtesy visit by Bin Laden and his lieutenants to an unidentified Sheikh, who appears crippled from the waist down. The visit apparently takes place at a guesthouse in Kandahar. The sequence of the events is reversed on the tape – the end of his visit is in the beginning of the tape with the helicopter site visit in the middle and the start of the Osama bin Laden visit beginning approximately 39 minutes into the tape. The tape is transcribed below according to the proper sequence of events.

Due to the quality of the original tape, it is NOT a verbatim transcript of every word spoken during the meeting, but does convey the messages and information flow.

Editor's Note: 39 minutes into tape, first segment of the bin Laden meeting, begins after footage of helicopter site visit.

Sheikh: (...inaudible...) *You have given us weapons, you have given us hope and we thank Allah for you. We don't want to take much of your time, but this is the arrangement of the brothers. People now are supporting us more, even those ones who did not support us in the past, support us more now. I did not want to take that much of your time. We praise Allah, we praise Allah.*

We came from Kabul. We were very pleased to visit. May Allah bless you both at home and the camp. We asked the driver to take us, it was a night with a full moon, thanks be to Allah. Believe me it is not in the country side. The elderly...everybody praises what you did, the great action you did, which was first and foremost by the grace of Allah. This is the guidance of Allah and the blessed fruit of jihad.

Osama bin Laden: *Thanks to Allah. What is the stand of the Mosques there* (in Saudi Arabia)*?*

Sheikh: *Honestly, they are very positive. Sheikh Al-Bahrani* (phonetic) *gave a good sermon in his class after the sunset prayers. It was videotaped and I was supposed to carry it with me, but unfortunately, I had to leave immediately.*

OBL: *The day of the events?*

Sheikh: *At the exact time of the attack on America, precisely at the time. He* (Bahrani) *gave a very impressive sermon. Thanks be to Allah for his blessings. He* (Bahrani) *was the first one to write at war time. I visited him twice in al-Qasim.*

OBL: *Thanks be to Allah.*

Sheikh: *This is what I asked from Allah. He* (Bahrani) *told the youth: "You are asking for martyrdom and wonder where you should go* (for martyrdom)*?" Allah was inciting them to go. I asked Allah to grant me to witness the truth in front of the unjust ruler. We ask Allah to protect him and give him the martyrdom, after he issued the first fatwah. He was detained for interrogation, as you know. When he was called in and asked to sign, he told them, "don't waste my time, I have another fatwah. If you want me, I can sign both at the same time."*

OBL: *Thanks be to Allah.*

Sheikh: *His position is really very encouraging. When I paid him the first visit about a year and half ago, he asked me, "How is Sheikh bin Laden?" He sends you his special regards. As far as Sheikh Suleiman Ulwan is concerned, he gave a beautiful fatwah, may Allah bless him. Miraculously, I heard it on the Koran radio station. It was strange because he* (Ulwan) *sacrificed his position, which is equivalent to a director. It was transcribed word-by-word. The brothers listened to it in detail. I briefly heard it before the noon prayers. He* (Ulwan) *said this was jihad and those people were not innocent people (World Trade Center and Pentagon victims). He swore to Allah. This was transmitted to Sheikh Suleiman al-* (Omar). *Allah bless him.*

OBL: *What about Sheikh al-* (Rayan)?

Sheikh: *Honestly, I did not meet with him. My movements were truly limited.*

OBL: *Allah bless you. You are welcome.*

Sheikh: (Describing the trip to the meeting) *They smuggled us and then I thought that we would be in different caves inside the mountains so I was surprised at the guest house and that it is very clean and comfortable. Thanks be to Allah, we also learned that this location is safe, by Allah's blessings. The place is clean and we are very comfortable.*

OBL: (...Inaudible...) *when people see a strong horse and a weak horse, by nature, they will like the strong horse. This is only one goal; those who want people to worship the lord of the people, without following that doctrine, will be following the doctrine of Muhammad, peace be upon him.*

(OBL quotes several short and incomplete Hadith verses, as follows):*"I was ordered to fight the people until they say there is no god but Allah, and his prophet Muhammad." "Some people may ask: why do you want to fight us?" "There is an association between those who say: I believe in one god and Muhammad is his prophet, and those who don't"* (...inaudible...) *"Those who do not follow the true fiqh. The fiqh of Muhammad, the real fiqh. They are just accepting what is being said at face value."*

OBL: *Those youth who conducted the operations did not accept any fiqh in the popular terms, but they accepted the fiqh that the prophet Muhammad brought. Those young men* (...inaudible...) *said in deeds, in New York and Washington, speeches that overshadowed all other speeches made everywhere else in the world. The speeches are understood by both Arabs and non-Arabs-even by Chinese. It is above all the media said. Some of them said that in Holland, at one of the centers, the number of people who accepted Islam during the days that followed the operations were more than the people who accepted Islam in the last eleven years. I heard someone on Islamic radio who owns a school in America say: "We don't have time to keep up with the demands of those who are asking about Islamic books to learn about Islam." This event made people think* (about true Islam) *which benefited Islam greatly.*

Sheikh: *Hundreds of people used to doubt you and few only would follow you until this huge event happened. Now hundreds of people are coming out to join you. I remember a vision by Sheikh Salih al-*(Shuaybi). *He said: "There will be a great hit and people will go out by hundreds to Afghanistan." I asked him* (Salih*): "To Afghanistan?" He replied, 'Yes." According to him, the only ones who stay behind will be the mentally impotent*

191

and the liars (hypocrites). I remembered his saying that hundreds of people will go out to Afghanistan. He had this vision a year ago. This event discriminated between the different types of followers.

OBL: (...Inaudible...) *we calculated in advance the number of casualties from the enemy, who would be killed based on the position of the tower. We calculated that the floors that would be hit would be three or four floors. I was the most optimistic of them all. (...Inaudible...) Due to my experience in this field, I was thinking that the fire from the gas in the plane would melt the iron structure of the building and collapse the area where the plane hit and all the floors above it only. This is all that we had hoped for.*

Sheikh: *Allah be praised.*

OBL: *We were at (...inaudible...) when the event took place. We had notification since the previous Thursday that the event would take place that day. We had finished our work that day and had the radio on. It was 5:30 p.m. our time. I was sitting with Dr. Ahmad Abu-al-(Khair). Immediately, we heard the news that a plane had hit the World Trade Center. We turned the radio station to the news from Washington. The news continued and no mention of the attack until the end. At the end of the newscast, they reported that a plane just hit the World Trade Center.*

Sheikh: *Allah be praised.*

OBL: *After a little while, they announced that another plane had hit the World Trade Center. The brothers who heard the news were overjoyed by it.*

Sheikh: *I listened to the news and I was sitting. We didn't... we were not thinking about anything, and all of a sudden, Allah willing, we were talking about how come*

*we didn't have anything, and all of a sudden the news
came and everyone was overjoyed and everyone until the
next day, in the morning, was talking about what was
happening and we stayed until four o'clock, listening to
the news every time a little bit different, everyone was
very joyous and saying "Allah is great," "Allah is
great," "We are thankful to Allah," "Praise Allah." And
I was happy for the happiness of my brothers. That day
the congratulations were coming on the phone non-stop.
The mother was receiving phone calls continuously.
Thank Allah. Allah is great, praise be to Allah.*

    (...)

    Sheikh: *No doubt it is a clear victory. Allah has
bestowed on us...honor on us...and he will give us blessing and more victory during this holy month of Rama-
dan. And this is what everyone is hoping for. Thank Allah
America came out of its caves. We hit her the first hit and
the next one will hit her with the hands of the believers,
the good believers, the strong believers. By Allah it is a
great work. Allah prepares for you a great reward for
this work. I'm sorry to speak in your presence, but it is
just thoughts, just thoughts. By Allah, who there is no
god but him. I live in happiness, happiness...I have not
experienced, or felt, in a long time. I remember, the
words of Al-Rabbani, he said they made a coalition
against us in the winter with the infidels like the Turks,
and others, and some other Arabs. And they surrounded
us like the days...in the days of the prophet Muhammad.
Exactly like what's happening right now. But he comforted his followers and said, "This is going to turn and hit
them back." And it is a mercy for us. And a blessing to
us. And it will bring people back. Look how wise he was.
And Allah will give him blessing. And the day will come*

when the symbols of Islam will rise up and it will be similar to the early days of al-Mujahedeen and al-Ansar (similar to the early years of Islam). And victory to those who follow Allah. Finally said, if it is the same, like the old days, such as Abu Bakr and Othman and Ali and others. In these days, in our times, that it will be the greatest jihad in the history of Islam and the resistance of the wicked people.

Sheikh: By Allah my Sheikh. We congratulate you for the great work. Thank Allah.

Tape ends here.

Second segment of bin Laden's visit, shows up at the front of the tape.

OBL: *Abdallah Azzam, Allah bless his soul, told me not to record anything (...inaudible...) so I thought that was a good omen, and Allah will bless us (...inaudible...). Abu-al-Hasan al-*(Masri), *who appeared on al-Jazeera TV a couple of days ago and addressed the Americans saying: "If you are true men, come down here and face us." (...inaudible...) He told me a year ago: "I saw in a dream, we were playing a soccer game against the Americans. When our team showed up in the field, they were all pilots!" He said: "So I wondered if that was a soccer game or a pilot game? Our players were pilots." He* (Abu-Al-Hasan) *didn't know anything about the operation until he heard it on the radio. He said the game went on and we defeated them. That was a good omen for us.*

Sheikh: *May Allah be blessed.*

Unidentified Man Off Camera: *Abd al Rahman*

al-(Ghamri) *said he saw a vision, before the operation, a plane crashed into a tall building. He knew nothing about it.*

Sheikh: *May Allah be blessed!*

Suleiman (Abu Guaith): *I was sitting with the Sheikh in a room, then I left to go to another room where there was a TV set. The TV broadcasted the big event. The scene was showing an Egyptian family sitting in their living room, they exploded with joy. Do you know when there is a soccer game and your team wins, it was the same expression of joy. There was a subtitle that read: "In revenge for the children of al-Aqsa', Osama bin Laden executes an operation against America." So I went back to the Sheikh* (meaning UBL) *who was sitting in a room with 50 to 60 people. I tried to tell him about what I saw, but he made gesture with his hands, meaning: "I know, I know..."*

OBL: *He did not know about the operation. Not everybody knew* (...inaudible...). *Muhammad* (Atta) *from the Egyptian family* (meaning the Egyptian al-Qaeda group), *was in charge of the group.*

Sheikh: *A plane crashing into a tall building was out of anyone's imagination. This was a great job. He was one of the pious men in the organization. He became a martyr. Allah bless his soul.*

Sheikh: (Referring to dreams and visions) *The plane that he saw crashing into the building was seen before by more than one person. One of the good religious people has left everything and come here. He told me, "I saw a vision, I was in a huge plane, long and wide. I was carrying it on my shoulders and I walked from the road to the desert for half a kilometer. I was dragging the plane." I listened to him and I prayed to*

Allah to help him. Another person told me that last year he saw, but I didn't understand and I told him I don't understand. He said, "I saw people who left for jihad...and they found themselves in New York...in Washington and New York." I said, "What is this?" He told me the plane hit the building. That was last year. We haven't thought much about it. But, when the incidents happened he came to me and said, "Did you see...this is strange." I have another man...my god...he said and swore by Allah that his wife had seen the incident a week earlier. She saw the plane crashing into a building...that was unbelievable, my god.

OBL: *The brothers, who conducted the operation, all they knew was that they have a martyrdom operation and we asked each of them to go to America but they didn't know anything about the operation, not even one letter. But they were trained and we did not reveal the operation to them until they are there and just before they boarded the planes.*

OBL: (...inaudible...) *then he said: Those who were trained to fly didn't know the others. One group of people did not know the other group.* (...inaudible...)

(Someone in the crowd asks OBL to tell the Shaeikh about the dream of (Abu-Daud).)

OBL: *We were at a camp of one of the brother's guards in Kandahar. This brother belonged to the majority of the group. He came close and told me that he saw, in a dream, a tall building in America, and in the same dream he saw Mukhtar teaching them how to play karate. At that point, I was worried that maybe the secret would be revealed if everyone starts seeing it in their dream. So I closed the subject. I told him if he sees another dream, not to tell anybody, because people will be upset with him.*

(Another person's voice can be heard recounting his dream about two planes hitting a big building).

OBL: *They were overjoyed when the first plane hit the building, so I said to them: be patient.*

OBL: *The difference between the first and the second plane hitting the towers was twenty minutes. And the difference between the first plane and the plane that hit the Pentagon was one hour.*

Sheikh: *They* (the Americans) *were terrified thinking there was a coup.*

[Note: Ayman al-Zawahri says first he commended OBL's awareness of what the media is saying. Then he says it was the first time for them (Americans) to feel danger coming at them.]

(Bin Laden recites a poem.)

Bin Laden visit footage complete. Footage of the visit to the helicopter site follows the poem. End of transcript

THE INCREDIBLE
NORTHWOODS OPERATION,

Or when American military officers wanted to organize "operations" on their own territory in order to present the invasion of Cuba as legitimate defense.

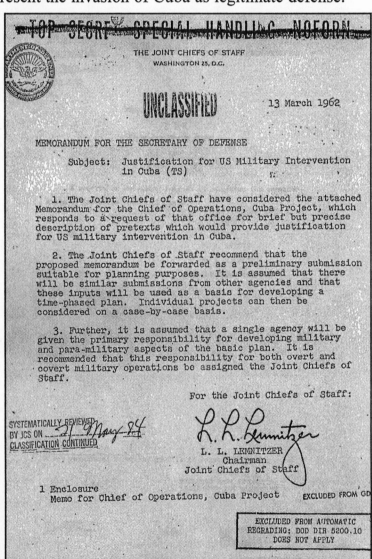

TOP SECRET SPECIAL HANDLING NOFORN

THE JOINT CHIEFS OF STAFF
WASHINGTON 25, D.C.

UNCLASSIFIED

13 March 1962

MEMORANDUM FOR THE SECRETARY OF DEFENSE

Subject: Justification for US Military Intervention in Cuba (TS)

1. The Joint Chiefs of Staff have considered the attached Memorandum for the Chief of Operations, Cuba Project, which responds to a request of that office for brief but precise description of pretexts which would provide justification for US military intervention in Cuba.

2. The Joint Chiefs of Staff recommend that the proposed memorandum be forwarded as a preliminary submission suitable for planning purposes. It is assumed that there will be similar submissions from other agencies and that these inputs will be used as a basis for developing a time-phased plan. Individual projects can then be considered on a case-by-case basis.

3. Further, it is assumed that a single agency will be given the primary responsibility for developing military and para-military aspects of the basic plan. It is recommended that this responsibility for both overt and covert military operations be assigned the Joint Chiefs of Staff.

For the Joint Chiefs of Staff:

L. L. LEMNITZER
Chairman
Joint Chiefs of Staff

SYSTEMATICALLY REVIEWED
BY JCS ON 21 May 84
CLASSIFICATION CONTINUED

1 Enclosure
Memo for Chief of Operations, Cuba Project   EXCLUDED FROM GD

EXCLUDED FROM AUTOMATIC
REGRADING; DOD DIR 5200.10
DOES NOT APPLY

TOP SECRET SPECIAL HANDLING NOFORN

DRAFT

MEMORANDUM FOR CHIEF OF OPERATIONS, CUBA PROJECT

Subject: Justification for US Military Intervention
          in Cuba (TS)

1. Reference is made to memorandum from Chief of Operations, Cuba Project, for General Craig, subject: "Operation MONGOOSE", dated 5 March 1962, which requested brief but precise description of pretexts which the Joint Chiefs of Staff consider would provide justification for US military intervention in Cuba.

2. The projects listed in the enclosure hereto are forwarded as a preliminary submission suitable for planning purposes. It is assumed that there will be similar submissions from other agencies and that these inputs will be used as a basis for developing a time-phased plan. The individual projects can then be considered on a case-by-case basis.

3. This plan, incorporating projects selected from the attached suggestions, or from other sources, should be developed to focus all efforts on a specific ultimate objective which would provide adequate justification for US military intervention. Such a plan would enable a logical build-up of incidents to be combined with other seemingly unrelated events to camouflage the ultimate objective and create the necessary impression of Cuban rashness and irresponsibility on a large scale, directed at other countries as well as the United States. The plan would also properly integrate and time phase the courses of action to be pursued. The desired resultant from the execution of this plan would be to place the United States in the apparent position of suffering defensible grievances from a rash and irresponsible government of Cuba and to develop an international image of a Cuban threat to peace in the Western Hemisphere.

5

Appendix to
Enclosure A

4. Time is an important factor in resolution of the Cuban problem. Therefore, the plan should be so time-phased that projects would be operable within the next few months.

5. Inasmuch as the ultimate objective is overt military intervention, it is recommended that <u>primary responsibility</u> for developing military and para-military aspects of the plan for both overt and covert military operations be assigned the Joint Chiefs of Staff.

Appendix to
Enclosure A

TOP SECRET — SPECIAL HANDLING — NOFORN

(Note: The courses of action which follow are a preliminary submission suitable only for planning purposes. They are arranged neither chronologically nor in ascending order. Together with similar inputs from other agencies, they are intended to provide a point of departure for the development of a single, integrated, time-phased plan. Such a plan would permit the evaluation of individual projects within the context of cumulative, correlated actions designed to lead inexorably to the objective of adequate justification for US military intervention in Cuba).

1. Since it would seem desirable to use legitimate provocation as the basis for US military intervention in Cuba a cover and deception plan, to include requisite preliminary actions such as has been developed in response to Task 33 c, could be executed as an initial effort to provoke Cuban reactions. Harassment plus deceptive actions to convince the Cubans of imminent invasion would be emphasized. Our military posture throughout execution of the plan will allow a rapid change from exercise to intervention if Cuban response justifies.

2. A series of well coordinated incidents will be planned to take place in and around Guantanamo to give genuine appearance of being done by hostile Cuban forces.

    a. Incidents to establish a credible attack (not in chronological order):

        (1) Start rumors (many). Use clandestine radio.

        (2) Land friendly Cubans in uniform "over-the-fence" to stage attack on base.

        (3) Capture Cuban (friendly) saboteurs inside the base.

        (4) Start riots near the base main gate (friendly Cubans).

Annex to Appendix
to Enclosure A

(5) Blow up ammunition inside the base; start fires.

(6) Burn aircraft on air base (sabotage).

(7) Lob mortar shells from outside of base into base. Some damage to installations.

(8) Capture assault teams approaching from the sea or vicinity of Guantanamo City.

(9) Capture militia group which storms the base.

(10) Sabotage ship in harbor; large fires -- napthalene.

(11) Sink ship near harbor entrance. Conduct funerals for mock-victims (may be lieu of (10)).

b. United States would respond by executing offensive operations to secure water and power supplies, destroying artillery and mortar emplacements which threaten the base.

c. Commence large scale United States military operations.

3. A "Remember the Maine" incident could be arranged in several forms:

a. We could blow up a US ship in Guantanamo Bay and blame Cuba.

b. We could blow up a drone (unmanned) vessel anywhere in the Cuban waters. We could arrange to cause such incident in the vicinity of Havana or Santiago as a spectacular result of Cuban attack from the air or sea, or both. The presence of Cuban planes or ships merely investigating the intent of the vessel could be fairly compelling evidence that the ship was taken under attack. The nearness to Havana or Santiago would add credibility especially to those people that might have heard the blast or have seen the fire. The US could follow up with an air/sea rescue operation covered by US fighters to "evacuate" remaining members of the non-existent crew. Casualty lists in US newspapers would cause a helpful wave of national indignation.

4. We could develop a Communist Cuban terror campaign in the Miami area, in other Florida cities and even in Washington.

The terror campaign could be pointed at Cuban refugees seeking haven in the United States. We could sink a boatload of Cubans enroute to Florida (real or simulated). We could foster attempts on lives of Cuban refugees in the United States even to the extent of wounding in instances to be widely publicized. Exploding a few plastic bombs in carefully chosen spots, the arrest of Cuban agents and the release of prepared documents substantiating Cuban involvement also would be helpful in projecting the idea of an irresponsible government.

5. A "Cuban-based, Castro-supported" filibuster could be simulated against a neighboring Caribbean nation (in the vein of the 14th of June invasion of the Dominican Republic). We know that Castro is backing subversive efforts clandestinely against Haiti, Dominican Republic, Guatemala, and Nicaragua at present and possible others. These efforts can be magnified and additional ones contrived for exposure. For example, advantage can be taken of the sensitivity of the Dominican Air Force to intrusions within their national air space. "Cuban" B-26 or C-46 type aircraft could make cane-burning raids at night. Soviet Bloc incendiaries could be found. This could be coupled with "Cuban" messages to the Communist underground in the Dominican Republic and "Cuban" shipments of arms which would be found, or intercepted, on the beach.

6. Use of MIG type aircraft by US pilots could provide additional provocation. Harassment of civil air, attacks on surface shipping and destruction of US military drone aircraft by MIG type planes would be useful as complementary actions. An F-86 properly painted would convince air passengers that they saw a Cuban MIG, especially if the pilot of the transport were to announce such fact. The primary drawback to this suggestion appears to be the security risk inherent in obtaining or modifying an aircraft. However, reasonable copies of the MIG could be produced from US resources in about three months.

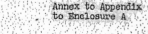

7. Hijacking attempts against civil air and surface craft should appear to continue as harassing measures condoned by the government of Cuba. Concurrently, genuine defections of Cuban civil and military air and surface craft should be encouraged.

8. It is possible to create an incident which will demonstrate convincingly that a Cuban aircraft has attacked and shot down a chartered civil airliner enroute from the United States to Jamaica, Guatemala, Panama or Venezuela. The destination would be chosen only to cause the flight plan route to cross Cuba. The passengers could be a group of college students off on a holiday or any grouping of persons with a common interest to support chartering a non-scheduled flight.

    a. An aircraft at Eglin AFB would be painted and numbered as an exact duplicate for a civil registered aircraft belonging to a CIA proprietary organization in the Miami area. At a designated time the duplicate would be substituted for the actual civil aircraft and would be loaded with the selected passengers, all boarded under carefully prepared aliases. The actual registered aircraft would be converted to a drone.

    b. Take off times of the drone aircraft and the actual aircraft will be scheduled to allow a rendezvous south of Florida. From the rendezvous point the passenger-carrying aircraft will descend to minimum altitude and go directly into an auxiliary field at Eglin AFB where arrangements will have been made to evacuate the passengers and return the aircraft to its original status. The drone aircraft meanwhile will continue to fly the filed flight plan. When over Cuba the drone will being transmitting on the international distress frequency a "MAY DAY" message stating he is under attack by Cuban MIG aircraft. The transmission will be interrupted by destruction of the aircraft which will be triggered by radio signal. This will allow ICAO radio

stations in the Western Hemisphere to tell the US what
has happened to the aircraft instead of the US trying to
"sell" the incident.

9. It is possible to create an incident which will make it
appear that Communist Cuban MIGs have destroyed a USAF aircraft
over international waters in an unprovoked attack.

    a. Approximately 4 or 5 F-101 aircraft will be dispatched
in trail from Homestead AFB, Florida, to the vicinity of Cuba.
Their mission will be to reverse course and simulate fakir
aircraft for an air defense exercise in southern Florida.
These aircraft would conduct variations of these flights at
frequent intervals. Crews would be briefed to remain at
least 12 miles off the Cuban coast; however, they would be
required to carry live ammunition in the event that hostile
actions were taken by the Cuban MIGs.

    b. On one such flight, a pre-briefed pilot would fly
tail-end Charley at considerable interval between aircraft.
While near the Cuban Island this pilot would broadcast that
he had been jumped by MIGs and was going down. No other
calls would be made. The pilot would then fly directly
west at extremely low altitude and land at a secure base, an
Eglin auxiliary. The aircraft would be met by the proper
people, quickly stored and given a new tail number. The
pilot who had performed the mission under an alias, would
resume his proper identity and return to his normal place
of business. The pilot and aircraft would then have
disappeared.

    c. At precisely the same time that the aircraft was
presumably shot down a submarine or small surface craft
would disburse F-101 parts, parachute, etc., at approximately
15 to 20 miles off the Cuban coast and depart. The pilots
returning to Homestead would have a true story as far as
they knew. Search ships and aircraft could be dispatched
and parts of aircraft found.

After his departure from Offutt Air Force Base, President Bush calls Vice President Cheney from Air Force One (9/11/01).

In the White House bunker, Vice President talks on the phone with President Bush. Condoleezza Rice is seated to the left (9/11/01).

White House photo by Paul Morse

President Bush during a visit to Elgin Air Force Base
(Florida) on 4 February 2002.

President Bush at the National Cathedral in Washington,
14 September 2001.

After his speech, President Bush shakes his father's hand.

Signing of the PATRIOT Act on 26 October 2001.

Colin Powell, President Bush, Dick Cheney and Hugh Shelton answer questions from the press at the White House on 12 September 2001.

Press conference at the Pentagon conducted by the Secretary of Defense, Donald H. Rumsfeld. It was on this occasion that a somewhat "heated" exchange took place with Senator Carl Levin (right) (9/11/01)

Press conference by Tom Ridge, Director of the Office of Homeland Security (10/18/01).

Meeting of the National Security Council (9/12/01).

Meeting in the Oval Office, with President Bush, and notably Governor Tom Ridge, Condoleeza Rice, Admiral Steve Abbot (12/20/01).

White House photo by Paul Morse

President Bush with Afghan Prime Minister Hami Karzai.

White House photo by Paul Morse

Prime Minister Hamid Kharzai receives
a standing ovation on 29 January 2002.

Department of the Air Force

General Ralph E. "Ed" Eberhart, Commander-in-Chief, North American Aerospace Defence Command and US Space Command; Commander, Air Force Space Command; and Department of Defense Manager for Manned Space Flight Support Operations, Petersen Air Force Base, Colorado.

Deputy Secretary of Defense Paul Wolfowitz.

DoD photo by R.D. Ward

NOTES

1 This statement was removed from the Department of Defense's Internet server. It can be consulted in the archives at the following University of Yale website: http://www.yale.edu/lawweb/avalon/sept_11/dod_brief03.htm
2 'Part of the Pentagon Collapses after Terrorists Crash Plane into Building', *Associated Press* dispatch, 11 September 2001.
3 'The Day the World Changed', *Christian Science Monitor*, 17 September 2001: http://www.csmonitor.com
4 'Inside the Pentagon Minutes before Raid', by Rick Pearson, *Chicago Tribune*, 12 September 2001: http://www.chicagotribune.com
5 *DoD News Briefing*, 12 September 2001, 3:35 p.m.
6 Special edition, *Christian Science Monitor*, 17 September 2001, downloadable from: http://www.csmonitor.com/pdf/csm20010917.pdf
7 Available at http://www.senate.gov/~armed_services
8 Available at http://www.peterson.af.mil/norad/presrelNO-RADTimelines.htm
9 Cf. *Public Report of the White House Security Review* (10 May 1995): http://www.fas.org/irp/agency/ustreas/usss/t1pubrpt.html
10 Official Website of Saint Andrews airbase: http://www.dcmilitary.com/baseguides/airforce/andrews
11 In *Newsday*, 23 September 2001.
12 According to information released by the constructor, Boeing: see http://www.boeing.com/commercial/757-200/product.html
13 A virtual tour of the Pentagon is available at http://www.defenselink.mil/pubs/pentagon
14 'Inside the Ring', an account by Bill Gertz, in the *Washing-*

ton Times, 21 September 2001: http://www.washtimes.com
15 Press conference led by the Deputy Defense Secretary, Victoria Clarke, Pentagon, 12 September 2001:
http://www.defenselink.mil/news/Sep2001/t09122001_t0912asd.html
16 'Nation's Capital Under State of Emergency', CNN, 12 September 2001: http://www.cnn.com (article originally located at :
http://www.cnn.com/2001/US/09/11/dc.terrorism/index.html)
17 Complete text available on the Egyptian presidential server:
http://www.presidency.gov.eg/html/14-Sept2001_press_2.html
18 'Up to 800 Possibly Dead at Pentagon' by James McIntyre & Matt Smith, *CNN*, 11 September, 2001:
http://www.cnn.com/2001/US/09/11/pentagon.terrorism/ ; and 'Three-Star General May Be Among Pentagon Dead', by Ian Christopher McCaleb, *CNN*, 13 September 2001:
http://www.cnn.com/2001/US/09/13/pentagon.terrorism/
19 'Get These Planes on the Ground', *ABC News*, 24 October, 2001:
http://www.abcnews.go.com/sections/2020/2020/2020_011024_act_feature.html ; and on the National Air Traffic Controllers Association (AFL-CIO) Website:
www.september11.natca.org/NewsArticles/DaniellOBrien.htm
20 Except on Flight 93 which exploded over Pennsylvania. The passengers on that flight indicated that the hijackers had a box which they said was a bomb.
21 That is, handguns made of synthetic materials that are not detectable at airport security gates: see for example http://www.glock.com
22 'Global Hawk, the DoD's Newest Unmanned Air Vehicle', DoD, February 1997:
http://www.defenselink.mil/photos/Feb1997/970220-D-0000G-001.html
23 '$elling Out the Investigation', by Bill Manning, *Fire Engineering*, January 2002. See also 'WTC Investigation? A Call for Action'(a petition published in the same issue of the review).

215

24 See, for example, the testimony of fireman Louie Cacchio-li (Brigade 47):
http://people.aol.com/people/special/0,11859,174592-3,00.html
25 'Explosives Planted in Towers, N.M. Tech Expert Says', by Olivier Uyttebrouck, *Albuquerque Journal*, 11 September 2001. Retraction in 'Fire, Not Extra Explosives, Doomed Buildings, Expert Says', by John Fleck, *Albuquerque Journal*, 21 September 2001: http://www.abqjournal.com
26 'Secret C.I.A. Site in New York Was Destroyed on Sept. 11', by James Risen, *The New York Times*, 4 November 2001: http://nytimes.com
27 We have learned of several testimonies according to which the CIA's base was located on floors 9 and 10 of tower 7. They used the New York Electronic Crime Task Force attached to the Secret Service as a cover. The same sources sent us photos of tower 7, taken after the collapse of the south tower, where one can clearly make out a fire on the ninth floor: http://members.aol.com/erichuf/eh_wtc16.jpg . We haven't been able to verify the authenticity of the photos or the veracity of this information.
28 'Final toll of World Trade Center is 2,843 Dead', *Associated Press* dispatch, 9 February 2002. This is the figure put forward by the city of New York. The press agency itself obtained a lower figure, 2,799 dead.
29 *Ha'aretz*, 26 September 2001: http://www.haaretzdaily.com/ . This information was repeated by Daniel Sieberg on CNN: 'FBI Probing "Threatening" Message, Firm Says', 28 September 2001: http://www.cnn.com . See also 'Instant Messages to Israel Warned of WTC Attack', by Brian McWilliams, *Newsbytes*, 27 September 2001; and 'Odigo Clarifies Attack Messages', by the same author, in the following day's edition: http://www.newsbytes.com . This information was broadcast in a distorted fashion by a commentator for Al-Jezeera, who tried to use it to support the thesis that the attacks were perpetrated by Mossad and that the latter had sent advance warning to Jewish employees in the WTC. The Qatari television net-

work immediately dismissed the journalist who concocted this story.

30 *A Force Upon the Plain: The American Militia Movement and the Politics of Hate*, by Kenneth Stern (Simon & Schuster, 1996). See also the first part of *The Secret Life of Bill Clinton: The Unreported Stories*, by Ambrose Evans-Pritchard (Regnery Publishing, 1997).

31 *Remarks by the President in Town Hall Meeting*, Orange County Convention Center, Orlando, Florida: http://www.whitehouse.gov/news/releases/2001/12/print/20011204-17.html

32 The United States Government Interagency Domestic Terrorism Concept of Operation Plan (CONPLAN), downloadable from http://www.fbi.gov/publications/conplan/conplan.pdf

33 The complete text is available at http://stacks.msnbc.com/news/629714.asp

34 Read in particular 'The Options', by Nicholas Lemann, *The New Yorker*, 25 September 2001: http://www.newyorker.com

35 For example: 'White House Said Targeted', by Sandra Sobieraj, *Washington Post*, 12 September 2001: http://www.washingtonpost.com ; and 'Inside the Bunker', *The New York Times,* 13 September 2001: http://www.nytimes.com

36 'Digital Codes in White House? Terrorists Had Top-Secret Presidential Codes', *World Ne tDaily*, 20 September 2001: http://www.worldnetdaily.com

37 'Bin Laden's Magic Carpet – Secret US Promis Software', Michael C. Ruppert, *From the Wilderness*, 20 November 2001: http://www.copvcia.com

38 Briefing by the Attorney General, John Ashcroft, 12 September 2001: http://www.usdoj.gov/ag/speeches/2001/0913pressconference.htm

39 Press conference by Attorney General John Ashcroft and FBI director Robert Mueller III, 14 September 2001: http://www.usdoj.gov/ag/agcrisisremarks9_14.htm

40 'Fighting the Forces of Invisibility', by Salman Rushdie,

Washington Post, 2 October 2001: http://www.washington-post.com

41 Briefing by the Attorney General, John Ashcroft, and the FBI director, Robert Mueller III, 28 September 2001: http://www.usdoj.gov/ag/agcrisisremarks9_28.htm

42 Several European newspapers mistakenly indicated that the FBI had discovered this document in the ruins at the Pentagon.

43 Curiously, the star reporter Bob Woodward pointed out this anomaly on the day it was published, but did not derive any conclusions. See 'In Hijacker's Bags, a Call to Planning, Prayer and Death, *Washington Post*, 28 September 2001: http://www.washingtonpost.com

44 'Saudi Minister Asserts That Bin Laden Is a "Tool" of Al Qaeda, Not a Mastermind', by Douglas Jehl, *New York Times*, 10 December 2001: http://www.nytimes.com

45 These press releases were circulated by the Associated Press agency.

46 *Black Tuesday: The World's Largest Insider Trading Scam?*, Don Radlauer, International Policy Institute for Counterterrorism, Israel, 19 September 2001: http://www.ict.org.il/articles/articledet.cfm?articleid=386

47 Official Website of IOSCO: http://www.iosco.org/iosco.html

48 'Suspicious Profits Sit Uncollected: Airlines Investors Seem to Be Lying Low', by Christian Berthelsen & Scott Winokur, *San Francisco Chronicle*, 29 September 2001: http://www.sfgate.com

49 *Révélation$*, by Denis Robert & Ernest Backes (Les Arènes, 2001): http://www.arenes.fr/livres/page-livre1.php?numero_livre=4&num_page=1

50 The FBI was also uninterested in identifying the owner of premonitory domain names on Internet: according to the registry company VeriSign, an unknown operator in 2000 bought for a year's period 19 Internet domain names, which would expire on 14 September 2001 and were never used. These were:

attackamerica.com, attackonamerica.com, attackontwinto-wers.com, august11horror.com, august11terror.com, horrorina-merica.com, horrorinnewyork.com, nycterroriststrike.com, pearlharborinmanhattan.com, terrorattack2001.com, towerof-horror.com, tradetowerstrike.com, worldtradecenter929.com, worldtradecenterbombs.com, worldtradetowerattack.com, worldtradetowerstrike.com, wterroristattack.com
See 'Internet Domain Names May Have Warned of Attacks', and 'Investigators Can Access Internet Domain Data', by Jeff Johnson, *CNS-News.Com*, 19 and 20 September 2001: http://www.CNS-News.com
51 *Statement by the President in His Address to the Nation*, 11 September 2001: http://www.whitehouse.gov/news/releases/2001/09/20010911-16.html
52 *The Trial of Henry Kissinger*, by Christopher Hitchens (Verso Books, 2001).
53 President Bush's speech started at 8:30 pm and Dr. Kissin-ger's views went online at 9:04 pm. 'Destroy the Network', by Henry Kissinger, *Washington Post*, 11 September 2001: http://washingtonpost.com
54 'Wednesday, September 12', by Bob Woodward & Dan Balz, *Washington Post*, 12 September 2002: http://www.washingtonpost.com
55 *Remarks by the President in Photo Opportunity with the National Security Team*, 12 September 2001: http://www.whi-tehouse.gov/news/releases/2001/09/20010912-4.html
56 *Resolution 1368*, Security Council, United Nations, 12 Sep-tember 2001, downloadable from : http://www.un.org/Docs/scres/2001/res1368e.pdf
57 *L'OTAN réaffirme les engagements pris au titre du Traité dans la réaction aux attaques terroristes contre les Etats-Unis*, Service de presse de l'OTAN, 12 September 2001: http://www.nato.int/docu/update/2001/0910/f0912a.htm
58 *UN Document SG/SM/7964*: http://www.un.org/News/fr-press/docs/2001/SGSM7964.doc.htm

59 Media briefing at FBI headquarters, 12 September 2001, 9:30 am

60 *DoD News Briefing*, 13 September 2001: http://www.defenselink.mil/news/Sep2001/t09132001_t0913d sd.html

61 'US Ask Pakistan for Help to Track Down Bin Laden', by Robin Wright & John Daniszewski, *Los Angeles Times*, 14 September 2001: http://www.latimes.com

62 'US Planned Attack on Taleban', *BBC*, 18 September 2001; and 'Secret Memo Reveals US Plan to Overthrow Taleban Regime', *Guardian*, 21 September 2001.

63 'A New Mindset for Warfare', by William M. Arkin, *Washington Post*, 22 September 2001: http://www.washing-tonpost.com

64 'God Gave US "What We Deserve"', Falwell Says', by John Harris, *Washington Post*, 14 September 2001: http://www.washingtonpost.com

65 *Proclamation by the President of the United States of America*, 13 September 2001: http://www.whitehouse.gov/news/releases/2001/09/20010913-7.html

66 For the American President, the two central dates around which the history of humanity orders itself are thus the birth of Jesus Christ and the birth of the United States, the one and the other being called to save the world.

67 *Billy Graham's Message*, 14 September 2001: http://www.billygraham.org/newsevents/ndprbgmessage.asp

68 *President's Remarks at National Day of Prayer and Remembrance*: http://www.whitehouse.gov/news/releases/2001/09/20010914-2.html

69 'Religious Right Finds Its Center in Oval Office', by Dana Millbank, *Washington Post*, 24 December 2001: http://www.washingtonpost.com

70 *800 millions d'Européens en deuil pour les victimes des attentats aux Etats-Unis*, communiqué of the Council of Euro-

pe, 13 September 2001 :
http://press.coe.int/ cp/2001/628f(2001).htm

71 *Remarks by the President in Photo Opportunity with the National Security Team*, 12 September 2001: http://www.whitehouse.gov/news/releases/2001/09/20010912-4.html

72 Décret NOR : HRUX0101919D, *Journal officiel de la République française*, 13 September 2001, p. 14582.

73 'War Speech in a Cathedral: A Steadfast Resolve to Prevail', by Dan Balz & Bob Woodward, *Washington Post*, 30 January 2002: http://washingtonpost.com

74 NATO = North American Treaty Organization; ANZUS allies Australia, New Zealand, and the United States; OAS = Organization of American States

75 'Le Nouvel arsenal de Washington dans l'infosphère', *Intelligence Online*, 14 February 2002 : http://www.intelligenceOnline.fr

76 The creation of the Bureau for Strategic Influence was the outcome of a long process of reflection by the American armed forces. Cf. 'Information Dominance', by Martin C. Libicki, *Strategic Forum* n° 132 (National Defense University, November 1997).

77 Official Website of International Information Programs: http://www.state.gov/r/iip

78 Since 1948, the State Department has a propaganda service modestly called " Public Diplomacy ". Its funding is used to corrupt opinion leaders (journalists, intellectuals, political figures) in friendly countries. By shifting these operations from the State Department to the Department of Defense, the Bush Administration extended the field of activity of the propaganda services to the U.S. population in violation of the Foreign Relations Authorizations Act of 1972.

79 Joint resolution 23 of Congress.

80 She explained her vote to her electors by publishing 'Why I Opposed the Resolution to Authorize Force', in the *San Francisco Chronicle*, 23 September 2001: http://sfgate.com

81 *National Emergency Powers*, by Harold C. Relyea,

Congressional Research Service, The Library of Congress, 18 September 2001: downloadable from :
http://www.fpc.gov/CRS_REPS/powers.pdf
82 'Congress Clears Use of Force, $40 Billion in Emergency Aid', by John Lancaster & Helen Dewar, *Washington Post*, 15 September 2001: http://www.washingtonpost.com ; and 'Congress Passes $40 Billion in Homeland Defense Funds', by Steven Kingsley, *Homeland Defense Journal*, 7 January 2002: http://www.homelanddefensejournal.com
83 Executive Order, 14 September 2001: http://www.white-house.gov/news/releases/2001/09/20010914-5.html
84 *Address to a Joint Session of Congress and the American People*, 20 September 2001:
http://www.whitehouse.gov/news/releases/2001/09/20010920-8.html
85 *DoD News Briefing, Secretary Rumsfeld*, 12 September 2001: http://www.defenselink.mil/news/Sep2001/t09122001-t0912sd.html
86 *DoD News Briefing, Secretary Rumsfeld*, 25 September 2001:
http://www.defenselink.mil/news/Sep2001/t09252001_t0925s d.html
87 Document available at
http://www.fas.org/sgp/news/2001/10/aldridge.html
88 Document available at
http://www.fas.org/sgp/news/2001/10/druyun.html
89 'Congressional Panels Join to Probe US Intelligence', by Walter Pincus, *Washington Post*, 12 September 2001: http://www.washingtonpost.com
90 'La "guerre de l'ombre" : les médias américains entre info et propagande', *Agence France Presse* dispatch, 11 October 2001.
91 Quoted by Olivier Pascal-Moussellard, in 'Les Journalistes à l'épreuve du 11 septembre', *Telerama*, 30 January 2002.
92 This extremely controversial provision was agreed to by the Democratic Party. Cf. the opinion piece by John Podesta (for-

mer White House chief of staff under Bil Clinton), 'Tools for Counterterrorism', *Washington Post*, 18 September 2001: http://www.washintonpost.com

93 *Attorney General Ashcroft Outlines Foreign Terrorist Tracking Task Force*, Department of Justice, 31 October 2001: http://www.usdoj.gov/ag/speeches/2001/agcrisisremarks10_31.htm

94 President's Military Order: *Detention, Treatment, and Trial of Certain Non-Citizens in War Against Terrorism*, 13 November 2001: http://www.whitehouse.gov/news/releases/2001/11/20011113-27.html

95 Official Website of the Counter-Terrorism Committee of the U.N. Security Council: http://www.un.org/Docs/sc/committees/1373/

96 Resolution 1373 of the Security Council, United Nations, 28 September 2001: downloadable from http://www.un.org/Docs/scres/2001/res1373e.pdf

97 See *Le Top 15 des Etats les plus liberticides*, by the Libertés immuables collective (Fédération internationale des ligues des Droits de l'homme, Human Rights Watch, Reporters sans frontières), downloadable from: http://www.enduring-freedoms.org/pdf/RAPPORTL.pdf

98 'The Threat to Patriotism', by Ronald Dworkin, *New York Review of Books*, 28 February 2002: http://www.nybooks.com

99 'Reviving a Misconceived Secrecy Bill' editorial, *New York Times*, 21 August 2001: http://www.newyorktimes.com ; 'No More Secrecy Bills', editorial, *Washington Post*, 24 August 2001: http://www.washingtonpost.com ; 'Classified Silencing', editorial, *St Petersburg Times*, 24 August 2001: http://www.sptimes.com ; 'No Official Secrets Act', editorial, *The Hill*, 5 September 2001: http://www.hillnews.com . Etc.

100 Task Force to Review Ways to Combat Leaks of Classified Information. Cf. 'Washington jaloux de ses sources ouvertes', *Intelligence Online*, 3 January 2002 : http://www.intelligenceOnline.fr

101 'Bush Names Army General to NSC Post on Terrorism', by Mike Allen & Thomas Ricks, *Washington Post*, 30 September 2001; and 'Two Key Advisers Are Filling New Posts to Fight New War', by Mike Allen & Eric Pianin, *Washington Post*, 10 October 2001: http://www.washingtonpost.com

102 *"Stay-behind"* is the most secret of the secret services. It was constituted during the Liberation of occupied territories in the Second World War, "turning" Nazi agents to fight against the growing influence of the Communists. Infiltrated at the highest levels of Western governments, it was utilized to manipulate the democratic process. The Italian branch of "stay behind" was known to the public under the name, *Gladio*.

103 *Homeland Security: The Presidential Coordination Office*, by Harold Relyea, Congressional Research Service, The Library of Congress, 10 October 2001: downloadable from http://www.fpc.gov/CRS_REP/crs_hsec.pdf

104 'Pentagon Debates Homeland Defense Role' by Bradley Graham & Bill Miller, *Washington Post*, 11 February 2002: http://www.washingtonpost.com

105 'The Emergence of the Fascist American Theocratic State', by John Stanton & Wayne Madsen, *Center for Globalisation Research*, 17 February 2002:
http://www.globalresearch.ca

106 Numerous works recount the biography of Osama bin Laden. Most of them owe more to propaganda or sensationalism than to rigorous investigation. The best-sellers such as *Bin Laden: The Man Who Declared War on America* by Yossef Bodansky (Prima Publishing, 1996) [Bodansky happens to be a consultant for Congress] or *Au nom d'Oussama Ben Laden* by Roland Jacquard (Jean Picollec, 2001) are based on unpublished reports from intelligence services, and are thus unverifiable. More serious are the investigations carried out by PBS's Frontline magazine, notably *Hunting Bin Laden* (2001) and *Inside the Terror Network* (2002). Full transcripts of the latter are available at:
http://www.pbs.org/wgbh/pages/frontline/shows

107 Cf. *Les Dollars de la terreur, les Etats-Unis et les isla-mistes*, by Richard Labérivière (Grasset, 1999); and *Jihad, expansion et déclin de l'islamisme*, by Gilles Kepel (Galli-mard, 2000).

108 Concerning the financial investments of Osama bin Laden, see *Ben Laden, La Vérité interdite*, by Jean-Charles Brisard & Guillaume Dasquié (Denoël, 2001).

109 *Hunting bin Laden*, Frontline (PBS, 2001): http://www.pbs.org/wgbh/pages/frontline/shows

110 *Meet the Press*, NBC, 23 September 2001: http://www.state.gov/secretary/rm/2001/index.cfm?docid=5012

111 *Responsibility for the Terrorist Atrocities in the United States, 11 September 2001*, by Tony Blair (first version): http://www.number-10.gov.uk/evidence.htm

112 Letter by Ambassador Negroponte to the president of the Security Council, UN Document S/2001/946. See also the let-ter from Ambassador Elton, UN Document S/2001/947.

113 *Responsibility for the Terrorist Atrocities in the United States, 11 September 2001*, by Tony Blair (second version). Downloadable from: http://www.pm.gov.uk/file.asp?fileid=2590

114 'New Tape Points to Bin Laden', by Walter Pincus & Karen DeYoung, *Washington Post*, 9 December 2001: http://www.washingtonpost.com

115 *This Week*, ABC, 9 December 2001.

116 The complete transcript of the cassette provided by the State Department is reproduced in the Appendices & Docu-ment section at the end of this book..

117 'The Masking of a Militant', by Benjamin Weiser & James Risen, *New York Times*, 1 December 1998.

118 *Terrorism: US Response to Bombing in Kenya and Tanza-nia, a New Policy Direction?*, by Raphael Perl, Congressional Research Service, Library of Congress, 1 September 1998: downloadable from http://www.house.gov/crstmp/98-733.pdf ; *Significant Incidents of POlitical Violence Against Americans*, State Department, 1998: downloadable from http://www.ds-

osac.org/publications/documents/sig1998.pdf

119 *Osamagate*, by Michael Chossudovsky, Center for Research on Globalisation, 9 October 2001: http://www.globalresearch.ca/articles/CHO110A.html ; and 'Les Soldats de Ben Laden en Bosnie et au Kosovo', by Kosta Christitch, *Balkans-Info*, October 2001.

120 'War on Terror Casts Chechen Conflict in a New Light', by Michael Wines, *New York Times*, 9 December 2001: http://nytimes.com

121 'La CIA a rencontré Ben Laden à Dubaï en juillet', by Alexandra Richard, *Le Figaro*, 31 October 2001.

122 'Hospital Worker: I Saw Osama', by Barry Petersen, *CBS*, 29 January 2002: http://www.cbsnews.com

123 'Terror Links to TV's Guarding UK', by Anthony Barnett & Conal Walsh, *The Observer*, 14 October 2001; and 'Inquiry Call Over Company Guarding UK Nuclear Plant', by the same authors, *The Observer*, 4 November 2001: http://www.observer.co.uk

124 *Pakistan's Inter-Service Intelligence*, by B. Raman, South Asia Analysis Group, Paper 287, 1 August 2001: http://www.saag.org

125 'India Helped FBI Trace ISI-Terrorist Link', *Times of India*, 9 October 2001: http://www.timesofindia.com

126 The BGM-109 Tomahawks were manufactured by General Dynamics in cooperation with McDonnell Douglas. They were billed to the American military for between 600,000 and 1.2 million dollars, depending on the model. The cost of munitions alone in this retaliatory strike was thus somewhere in the range of 45 to 90 million dollars.

127 'Qui est Oussama Ben Laden ?', by Michel Chossudovsky, *L'Autre Journal*, October 2001, article reproduced at http://www.globalresearch.ca/articles/CHO109E.html

128 We have dealt in detail with these relations in 'Les Liens financiers occultes des Bush et des Ben Laden', *Notes d'informations du Réseau Voltaire*, 16 October 2001. This investigation was re-published in Mexico by *Proceso* under the title

'Lazos que unen a las familias Bush y Bin Laden:
http://www.proceso.commx/1303/1303n19.html
129 'John Major Link to Bin Laden Dynasty', *Sunday Herald*, 7 October 2001.
130 'Bush of Arabia', *The Nation*, 27 March 2000; and 'Elder Bush in Big GOP Cast Toiling for Top Equity Firm', *New York Times*, 5 March 2001
131 Harken Energy Corporation was originally called Arbusto.
132 'Fuel for Fantasy', *Forbes*, 3 September 1990; and 'Ex-Bush Aide Turns to Stumping for Kuwait... While Jr. Reaps Oil Windfall', *The Guardian*, 12 December 1990.
133 The BCCI scandal has been the subject of abundant literature. We referred above all to *The BCCI Affair*, a report by Sen. Joseph Kerry (D-Mass.) and Sen. Hank Brown (R-Colo.) to the Senate Committee on Foreign Relations, Subcommittee on Terrorism, Narcotics and International Operations, 30 September 1992. Complete text available at:
http://www.fas.org/irp/congress/1992-rpt/bcci .. See also *Evil Money, Encounters Along the Money Trail*, by Rachel Ehrenfeld (Harper Business, 1992); *False Profits: The Inside Story of BCCI, the World's Most Corrupt Financial Empire*, by Peter Truell & Larry Gurwin (Houghton, 1992); *A Full Service Bank: How the BCCI Stole Billions Around the World* (Simon & Schuster, 1992); *The Outlaw Bank: A Wild Ride Into the Secret Heart of BCCI*, by Jonathan Beaty & S.C. Gwynne (Random House, 1993); and *Bankrupt: The BCCI Fraud*, by Nick Kochan & Bob Whittington (Victor Gollancz, 1991).
134 The French agent of Gaith Pharaon, Farid Djouri, bought two pages of advertising in *Le Figaro* and *Le Monde* in October 2001. This communications campaign aimed at denying any links between Gaith Pharaon and Osama bin Laden, and to defend the integrity of the former. Gaith Pharaon is the object of a FBI and IRS arrest warrant since the BCCI affair. He was also implicated in a arms traficking scandal in Argentina that also involved former President Carlos Menem. Cf. 'Gaith Pharaon s'offre la presse française', *Intelligence Online*, 18 Octo-

ber 2001 : http://www.intelligenceOnline.fr

135 *Adnan Khashoggi: The Richest Man in the World*, by Ronald Kessler (Warner Books, 1986).

136 *L'Enigma Pasqua*, by Thierry Meyssan (Golias, 2001).

137 Initially, SICO was called CYGNET.

138 *Presidential Address to the Nation*, 7 October 2001: http://www.whitehouse.gov/news/releases/2001/10/20011007-8.html

139 'Texte de la déclaration d'Oussama Ben Laden', *Agence France Presse* dispatch, 7 October 2001

140 The expression "the Great Game" came back into fashion with articles by Ahmed Rashid in the *Far Eastern Economic Review*. See *The New Great Game in Muslim Central Asia*, by M. Ehsan Ahrari, McNair Paper n°47 (National Defense University, 1996): downloadable from: http://www.ndu.edu/inss/macnair/macnair47.pdf ; *Central Asia: A New Great Game?*, by Dianne L. Smith (US Army War College, 1996): downloadable from http://carlisle-www.army.mil/usassi/ssipubs/pubs96/centasia/centasia.pdf ; *The New Great Game: Oil, Politics in the Caucasus and Central Asia* (Heritage Foundation, 1996); *Jihadi Groups, Nuclear Pakistan, and the New Great Game*, by Ehsan Ahrari (US Army War College, 2001): downloadable from http://carlisle-www.army.mil/usassi/ssipubs/pubs2001/jihadi/jihadi.pdf . See also *Les Rivalités autour du pétrole de la mer Caspienne*, by Comité 4 de la 51e session de l'Institut des Hautes Etudes de la Défense nationale, 1999 : http://www.ihedn.fr

141 *Taliban and the Drug Trade*, by Raphael F. Perl, Congressional Research Service, Library of Congress, 5 October 2001: downloadable at http://www.fpc.gov/CRS_REPS/crstalib.pdf ; and *Central Asia: Drugs and Conflict*, by the International Crisis Group: http://www.crisis-web.org/projects/asia/centralasia/reports/A400495_26112001-2.pdf

142 'Critics Knock Naming Oil Tanker Condoleezza', by Carla Marinucci, *San Francisco Chronicle*, 5 April 2001.

143 Mrs. Rice was an administrator and shareholder of Che-

vron until her appointment to the National Security Council. Chevron is the new name of the firm founded by John D. Rockefeller, Standard Oil of California, also known as Esso Standard. Chevron and Texaco merged on 9 October 2001: http://www.ChevronTexaco.com . With 112 billion dollars in turnover, the new company is the second largest US multinational, behind Exxon-Mobil (218 billion dollars in turnover).

144 BP (British Petroleum)-Amoco is the third largest oil group in the world with a turnover of 157 billion dollars: http://bp.com . BP-Amoco merged some of its services in Europe with Mobil.

145 Official Website: http://www.halliburton.com/ . With a turnover of 11.5 billion dollars, Halliburton is the biggest supplier of equipment to the petroleum industry, ahead of Schlumberger (9 billion euros in turnover).

146 'Energy Task Force Works in Secret', by Dana Milbank & Eric Pianin, *Washington Post,* 16 April 2001: http://www.washingtonpost.com

147 In order successfully carry out this project, UNOCAL at first created the consortium Central Asia Gas (called CentGas) with Delta Oil, Gazprom, and Turkmenogaz. It came up against unexpected competition from the Argentine group, Bridas. Then it set up the Central Asian Oil Pipeline Project with the Saudi company Delta Oil, the government of Turkmenistan, Indonesian Petroleum (INPEX), the Japanese company ITOCHU, Hyundai from Korea, and the Pakistani Crescent Group.

148 See *L'Ombre des Talibans*, by Ahmed Rashid (Autrement, 2001).

149 Declaration of the ministerial spokesperson, press conference, French Ministry of Foreign Affairs, 17 July 2001: http://www.diplomatie.gouv.fr/actual/declarations/pp/2001071 7.html

150 Official Website of the Business Humanitarian Forum: http://www.bhforum.org

151 Video interview with Niz Naik by Benoît Califano, Pierre

Trouillet and Guilhem Rondot (ITV-Dokumenta co-production, October 2001), not broadcast.

152 The assassination of Shah Massoud was kept secret for several days and only revealed after the attacks in the United States. It was then attributed to Osama bin Laden. The current version of his death does not in fact correspond at all with the testimony gathered soon after by French journalist Françoise Causse. At the time, the followers of Shah Massoud tended to pin blame on the Pakistani secret services.

153 The best synthetic overviews of "Enduring Freedom" are those of the British Parliament's research unit: *11 September 2001, the Response* (Research Paper 01/72, 3 October 2001); *Operation Enduring Freedom and the Conflict in Afghanistan, an Update* (Research Paper 01/81, 31 October 2001); and *The Campaign Against International Terrorism, Prospects After the Fall of the Taliban* (Research Paper 01/112). These documents are respectively downloadable at :

http://www.parliament.uk/commons/lib/research/rp2001/rp01-072.pdf ;

http://www.parliament.uk/commons/lib/research/rp2001/rp01-081.pdf ;

http://www.parliament.uk/commons/lib/research/rp2001/rp01-112.pdf

154 For an analysis of commitments, state by state, cf. *Operation Enduring Freedom: Foreign Pledges of Military & Intelligence Support*, Congressional Research Service, Library of Congress, 17 October 2001: downloadable at http://www.fpc.gov/CRS_REPS/crs-free.pdf .

155 *The Global War on Terrorism, The First 100 Days*, official document of the Coalition Information Center: downloadable at http://www.whitehouse.gov/news:releases/2001/12/100day-report.pdf

156 *Agence France Presse* dispatch, 6 December 2001.

157 *Operation Enduring Freedom: Why a Higher Rate of Civilian Bombing Casualties*, Project on Defense Alternatives, Briefing Report #11, 18 January 2002:

http://www.comw.org/pda/0201oef.html ; 'US Silence and Power of Weaponry Conceal Scale of Civilian Toll', *Sydney Morning Herald*, 26 January 2002: http://www.smh.comau ; 'Afghans Are Still Dying as Air Strikes Go On, But No One Is Counting', by Ian Traynor, *Guardian*: http://www.guardian.co.uk ; and 'Civilian Toll in US Raids Put at 1,000', by John Donnelly & Anthony Shadid, *Boston Globe*, 17 February 2002: http://www.boston.com/globe

158 The BLU-82's were not initially conceived for use in combat, as the damage they cause is too great and too indiscriminate, but for engineering purposes. They were used in Vietnam to clear the jungle and prepare landing zones for helicopters;

159 Security Council 1378: downloadable at : http://www.un.org/Docs/scres/2001/res1378e.pdf

160 Official Website of the Bonn talks: http://www.uno.de/frieden/afghanistan/talks.htm ; Text of the Bonn Accord: downloadable at: http://www.uno.de/frieden/afghanistan/talks/agreement.pdf

161 *Strange Victory: A Critical Appraisal of Operation Enduring Freedom and the Afghanistan War*, by Carl Conetta, Project on Defense Alternatives, monograph #6, 30 January 2002: http://www.comw.org/pda/0201strangevic.html

162 'Afghanistan, the Taliban and the Bush Oil Team', by Wayne Madsen, *Democrats.Com*, 23 January 2002: http://www.democrats.com

163 Security Council Resolution 1383: downloadable at http://www.un.org/Docs/scres/2001/res1383e.pdf

164 'The Roving Eye/Pipelineistan', investigation in two parts by Pepe Escobar, *Asia Times*, 25 and 26 January 2002: http://atimes.com

165 See his portrait in 'Bush's Favorite Afghan', by Jacob Weisberg, *Slate*, 5 October 2001: http://slate.msm.com ; and 'New US Envoy to Kabul Lobbied for Taliban Oil Rights', by Kim Sengupta & Andrew Gumbel, *The Independent*, 10 January 2002: http://www.independent.co.uk . Zalmay Khalilzad's views deserve special attention, cf. *Speech before the Los*

Angeles World Affairs Council, 9 March 2000: http://www.lawac.org/speech/khalilzad.html ; and an article co-written with Daniel Byrman, 'Afghanistan: The Consolidation of a Rogue State', *Washington Quarterly*, Winter 2000.

166 'Opium Farmers Rejoice at Defeat of the Taliban', by Richard Lloyd Parry, *Independent*, 21 November 2001: http://www.independent.co.uk ; and 'Victorious Warlords Set to Open the Opium', by Paul Harris, *The Observer*, 25 November 2001: same URL as *The Guardian*: http://www.guardian.co.uk)

167 'Musharraf, Karzai Agree Major Oil Pipeline in Co-Operation Pact', *Irish Times*, 9 February 2002: http://ireland.com

168 'Maintaining Public Support for Military Operations', by L. Wong, *Defeating Terrorism, Strategic Issues Analysis* (Strategic Studies Institute): downloadable at http://carlisle-www.army.mil/usassi/public.pdf

169 *Is the FBI Dragging Its Feet?*, by Barbara Hatch Rosenberg, Federation of American Scientists, 5 February 2002: http://www.fas.org/bwc/news/anthraxreport.htm

170 Concerning the controversy over this issue, see *Trying Terrorists as War Criminals*, by Jennifer Elsea, Congressional Research Service, Library of Congress, 29 October 2001: downloadable at : http://www.fpc.gov/CRS_REPS/trying%20terrorists.pdf

171 Guantanamo was ceded to the United States for ninety-nine years by the newly independent Republic of Cuba following the Spanish-American War. The lease was not renewed by Fidel Castro when it came to term. Nevertheless, the United States have not evacuated Guantanamo and continue to occupy the base illegally. Under international law, Cuban legislation should be applicable on the base's territory, but the Cuban government is unable to exercise its authority there.

172 'L'Autre sale guerre d'Aussaresses', by Pierre Abramovici, *Le Point*, 15 July 2001 ; and 'The French Connection in the Export of Torture', by César Chelala, *International Herald Tribune*, 22 June 2001.

173 *Déclaration de la Haute-commissaire aux Droits de l'homme sur la détention de prisonniers et d'Al-Qaeda à Guantanamo*, United Nations, Document HR/02/4, 16 January 2002 : http://www.unhcr

174 'Negroponte entre à l'ONU sur un vote unanime du Sénat', by Guy Allard, *Gramma International*, October 2001.

175 'Saturday, September 15, at Camp David, Advise and Dissent', by Bob Woodward & Dan Balz, *Washington Post*, 31 January 2002: http://www.washingtonpost.com

176 'J'Accuse – Bush's Death Squads', by Wayne Madsen, *MakingNews.Com*, 31 January 2002.

177 'Death of a Patriot', *Newswatch*, 30 December 2001: http://www.newswatchngr.com

178 'Elie Hobeika, le choc d'un assassinat'; and 'Détails exclusifs sur l'attentat', *L'Hebdo Magazine*, 22 February 2002 : http://www.magazine.com.lb

179 'Phase II and Iraq', by Henry Kissinger, *Washington Post*, 13 February 2002: http://www.washingtonpost.com

180 'Interview with Hubert Védrine', *Question directe,* France Inter radio, 6 February 2002: http://www.diplomatie.fr

181 *Allocution du Premier ministre devant la Conférence des présidents des Parlements de l'Union européenne contre le blanchiment d'argent*, Assemblée nationale, 8 February 2002 : http://www.premier-ministre.fr

182 'Breaking the Silence', interview with Chris Patten, *Guardian*, 9 February 2002: http://www.guardian.co.uk

183 'Chretien Resists American Pressure on Iraq', by Sandra Cordon, *Halifax Herald*, 18 February 2002: http://Herald.ns.ca ; and 'US Worries About PM's Position on Fighting Iraq', by Daniel Leblanc, *Toronto Globe and Mail*, 18 February 2002: http://GlobeandMail.com

184 *A Program of Covert Operations Against the Castro Regime*, declassified CIA document dated 16 April 1961.

185 *The Chairmen of the Joint Chiefs of Staff*, by Willard J. Webb & Ronald H. Cole (DoD, 1989); and *Swords and Plowshares*, by Maxwell D. Taylor, 1972.

186 See our study 'Les Forces spéciales clandestines' in *Les Notes d'information du Réseau Voltaire* n°235. For more ample details, see *Edwin A. Walker and the Right Wing in Dallas*, by Chris Cravens (South Texas University, 1993).

187 Since the end of the Korean war, Major General Edwin Walker was convinced that the US government was engaged in a policy of abandonment vis-a-vis the Communist threat. After being relieved of his duties by the Secretary of Defense, Robert McNamara, and receiving a reprimand, he provoked a riot at the University of Mississippi to protest against the hiring of a black professor. He was then prosecuted by the Attorney General, Robert Kennedy, and arrested for seditious conspiracy, insurrection, and rebellion. Supported by the conservative press who called him the "Kennedys' political prisoner', he was released from jail after posting one hundred thousand dollars in bail. He was later discovered to be funding a plot by the Organisation armée secrète (OAS : an extremist pro-French Algeria movement) to assassinate French President Charles de Gaulle, and then was involved in the "8F Committee" suspected of having planned the assassination of JFK.

188 *The Secret Surrender*, by Allen Dulles (Harper & Row, 1966).

189 The documents of the Northwoods operation were initially published in Australia by Jon Elliston (*Psy War on Cuba: The Declassified History of US Anti-Castro Propaganda*, Ocean Press, 1999) without raising reactions in the United States. They were used again as a source by the ABC news journalist, James Bamford, in his history of the NSA (*Body of Secrets: Anatomy of the Ultra-Secret National Security Agency from the Cold War to the Dawn of a New Century*, Doubleday, 2001), which aroused considerable excitement among historians.

190 At that time, Cuba was a Spanish colony. The USA intervened militarily to complete the decolonization of Cuba and to impose the status of protectorate upon the island.

191 The surveillance of airspace is such that it would be diffi-

cult today to switch planes without controllers noticing the hoax. But it is not impossible, however. It's known that each airliner has a transponder that transmits an identification signal and flight data (altitude, speed, etc.), so that the controllers do not see a point on their radar screens, but the plane's registration. Nevertheless, the exact knowledge of airspace is protected by military secrecy, where civilian radars are equipped with a filter that blinds them when they detect airplanes whose transponders emit military codes. To switch planes, you would need to possess a military code and cut off the civilian transponder during the switch.

You will note that on September 11, the transponders of the four planes officially hijacked stopped transmitting for an unknown reason. According to the procedure currently in effect, the air traffic controllers should immediately establish radio contact to verify that the plane is not in distress, and failing that, warn the military authorities (NORAD) so that they can establish visual contact from their fighters.

192 *Farewell Address*, by Dwight Eisenhower, 17 January 1961.

193 *JFK: Autopsie d'un crime d'Etat,* by Walter Reymond (Flammarion, 1998)

194 *Terrorism in the United States*, FBI: downloadable at
1996: http://www.fbi.gov/publications/terror/terroris.pdf ;
1997: http://www.fbi.gov/publications/terror/terr97.pdf ;
1998: http://www.fbi.gov/publications/terror/terror98.pdf ;
1999: http://www.fbi.gov/publications/terror/terror99.pdf

195 This affair was the subject of four articles by Nick Pron in the *Toronto Star*: 'Did This Man Predict Sept. 11?' (23 October 2001); 'US Looks into Inmate's Story, Jail Man Said He Tried to Warn About Attacks' (25 October); 'Plot to Murder Judge May Never Have Existed' (31 October); and 'Was Embassy Worker Poisoned?' (21 January 2002): http://www.thestar.com

The third article also makes reference to testimony concerning the murder of a judge. The change of attitude of the police in this other affair seems to be utilized as an attempt to discredit Vreeland. In addition, Michael Ruppert, the editor of *From the Wilderness*, who is in contact with Vreeland's lawyers, has devoted several articles to this affair at http://copvcia.com

196 Hearing on 26 September 2001: http://www.rand.org/publications/CT/CT182/CT182.pdf

197 Official Website of the Rand Corporation: http://www.rand.org

198 'Twenty-First Century Terrorism', in *The Terrorism Threat and US Government Response: Operational and Organizational Factors*, US Air Force Academy, Institute for National Security Studies, March 2001. Bruce Hoffman's text is available at http://www.usafa.af.mil/inss/foreword.htm

199 *Report of the Commission to Assess U.S. National Security Space Management and Organization:* http://www.defenselink.mil/pubs/space2001011.html

200 *DoD News Briefing on Pentagon Attack*: http://www.defenselink.mil/cgi-bin/dlprint.cgi

201 *America's Holy War*, by William S. Cohen, *Washington Post*, 12 September 2001: http://www.washingtonpost.com

202 The complete text of the interview is available at http://stacks.msnbc.com/news/629714.asp

203 'State Sponsors of Terrorism Should Be Wiped Out, Too', by Richard Perle, *Daily Telegraph*, 18 September 2001: http://www.dailytelegraph.co.uk

204 'A New Kind of War', by Donald Rumsfeld, *Washington Post*, 27 September 2001: http://www.washingtonpost.com

205 Highlighted in bold by us.

206 'Martial Justice, Full and Fair', by Alberto Gonzales, *New York Times*, 30 November 2001: http://nytimes.com

TABLE OF CONTENTS

Page

PART I
A BLOODY STAGE IS SET

PART II
THE DEATH OF DEMOCRACY IN AMERICA

PART III
THE EMPIRE ATTACKS

ACKNOWLEDGEMENTS

The author would like to thank A.-J. V. and G.S. who offered to verify the translations of various documents and quotations; E.B., P.-H. B., F.C., S.J., M.-V., for their expertise; A.B.,C.B., J.C., B.C., C.C., C.D., M.M., R.M., R.-J.P., E.R., D.S. for their documentary assistance; and above all Serge Marchand who coordinated the entire research and preparatory work.